THE LIGHTHOUSE COOKBOOK

THE LIGHTHOUSE COOKBOOK

Anita Stewart

Harbour Publishing

First paperback edition 1994

THE LIGHTHOUSE COOKBOOK
Copyright © 1988 by Anita Stewart

HARBOUR PUBLISHING CO. LTD.
P.O. Box 219
Madeira Park, BC
V0N 2H0

Edited by Mary Schendlinger
Cover and text design: Fiona MacGregor
Cover photo: Mike Gluss
Drawings of Carmanah Point, Entrance Island, Estevan Point, Lennard Island, Pachena Point, Point Atkinson, Quatsino and Race Rocks by Gaye Hammond; drawings of Ballenas, Cape Mudge, Egg Island, Green Island, Ivory Island, Langara Point, Merry Island, Pine Island, Pointer Island, Scarlett Point and Sisters Island by Donna Williams.

Printed and bound in Canada by Friesen Printers

Canadian Cataloguing in Publication Data

Stewart, Anita.
    The lighthouse cookbook

    ISBN 1-55017-103-8

    1. Cookery, Canadian — British Columbia
style.   2. Cookery (Seafood).   3. Lighthouses —
British Columbia.   I. Title.
TX715.S84 1988   641.59711′3   C88-091381-9

For all the families who keep British Columbia's lights shining. And for my own, who kept the homefires burning.

Special Thanks

To Mike Gluss... for continually pestering me with new ideas!

To Captains Bob Mellis and Fred "Fairweather" Wedgewood, and the superb crews, the men and women of both the CCGS *Martha L. Black* and the CCGS *George R. Pearkes*. Your professionalism is a credit to our country.

To Rex "Pen" Brown of Victoria and Vivian Skinner of Prince Rupert Coast Guard Bases. Without your organizational abilities I would still be somewhere on the shore. Your love of the lights is contagious!

To the Ocean Centre and Tim Bragg of Victoria for helping me make the spectacular dives at Race Rocks. And to Sinclair, my diving buddy.

To my family, Wayne, Jeff, Brad, Mark and Paul... for being the guinea pigs for yet another series of recipe testings... and for bearing up while I was away, sloshing about in the distant Pacific.

Contents

Introduction

Food and life and love, they are inseparable. The way we eat and drink reflects the way we are...Canadians, British Columbians, lightkeepers.

This book offers a glimpse of a Canadian way of life and its foodways which, despite the protesting chorus, may eventually be lost. Although the "demanning" process has been stalled, it has not been stopped altogether. Many of the lights are going, some in this book are gone!

The lightstations of British Columbia are unique to North America. With the exception of a few lights protecting the rugged coast of Newfoundland, all the others across the nation are situated so that the keepers drive to them, work their shift and then return home to their families. The Americans have automated all their lights so that the role of the keepers has been reduced to mainly grass-cutting chores.

In September 1986, I was on an assignment for *Canadian Living* at Steveston's Fisherman's Market. Among the crowds of the busy fishing dock, I met Mike Gluss, a photographer from Saltspring Island who was there to take location shots. Mike and I hit it off right away...he is easily as crazy as I am. The afternoon of shooting various strange bottom fish, their jaws gaping, ended with the two of us sitting in Mike's van drinking brandied coffee topped with squirts of whipped cream (a true photographer always comes prepared) as the sun slowly cooled in the western sky. And we talked about Canada. He was about to set off on a nation-wide photographic odyssey and I was drugged with the beauty of the Pacific coast (the coffee helped too). It was during that brief meeting that he told me the saga of the lightkeepers and how, at that moment, they were fighting for their existence. Without Mike, this book would never have been written.

In May 1987, I was to board CCGS *George R. Pearkes*, or so I thought—anyway, my baggage did. I was shuttled to the helicopter pad where C. J. Simpson, a veteran chopper pilot and Glen, his inscrutable engineer, were waiting. We were to visit Race Rocks before landing on the ship...landing on the ship?!?! It's hard to act cool when 1) you've never had the dubious privilege of flying in a helicopter, 2) you've never flown over the ocean at less than 20,000 feet, and 3) you've no idea what credentials these two, shall we say "characters," have. But we survived, dipsey-doodling above Race and finally, without a shiver, onto the deck of the *Pearkes*, while she pounded through swells and hobby-horsed on their crests. It was my first hair-raising encounter with our Coast Guard and it was not to be my last.

From being a meek, mild-mannered housewife, I became adept at swinging over the side of a rolling icebreaker, down rope ladders and into rollercoasting work boats. Believe me, that manoeuvre in itself is a feat. I saw one young agile crew member fall spread-eagled into the chilling water after losing his slippery footing. With the helping hands of the crew I learned how not to imitate his ignominious display.

During that trip, which circumnavigated Vancouver Island, and later in the year on the CCGS *Martha L. Black* in the northern district of Prince Rupert, I visited the last of the twenty-eight lightstations that are represented in this book. I landed on most of the southern stations via Messerschmidt helicopter. But in the north, I made the trips ashore in a work boat that was pushing a 17,000 litre fuel barge or in a gutsy little zodiac. Wearing a bright orange survival suit and rubber boots that always seemed to gurgle with sea water, I was welcomed with open arms, steaming mugs of coffee and plates of cookies, squares and cakes. Never, in all my travels as a foodie, have I encountered such a consistently excellent group of cooks as on the lightstations of British Columbia.

Once a month food arrives. Sometimes it's lightly dropped by helicopter, but most often it is loaded into deep work boats and sloshed ashore by the crew. Winches and pullies help to sling the monthly supplies, sometimes sodden, onto the cement pads where, as quickly as possible, they are stored safely away. The grocery bills range from $400 to $700 per month and most stations have a storeroom that has a few months' supplies ahead, in case of emergency. Flour and many other staples are purchased from the wholesaler in bulk, to be dumped into big plastic storage buckets.

With limited freezer space—indeed, freezers have only been available for the past twenty years or so—the families of the lights have to be pioneers in the truest sense. They are left to their own devices. And those who are resourceful survive in a wonderful way—freshly baked breads, home-grown vegetables, the ultimate in just-harvested shellfish, wild game, and an incomparable chance to touch the earth.

But lightkeeping is much, much more. It's young Judy marrying Gorden Schweers in the flowered meadow of Nootka Sound—the spot where BC's modern history began. It's Karen Coldwell walking the trails of Pachena that her grandfather, a linesman, helped to clear. It's Etta and Matt Martinelli teaching their sons a course of study that they developed themselves. It's Dan and Fil McMurray grinding the wheat for their bread in a flour mill he built. It's young Guthrie's paintings of whales and boats and the sea posted on the walls of the Prince Rupert Coast Guard office.

Lightkeeping is the commitment to build a good life—the magnificent stone greenhouse at Ivory Island, a microphone listening for the undersea singing of whales at Boat Bluff. It's the peregrine falcons of Langara and the hummingbirds of Scarlett Point.

It's also a life of danger and darkness, lost at sea bulletins and tsunami warnings. Weeks creep by without a break from the relentless pounding of rain and the winter surf. Gale follows hard on gale. The skies ooze. Fishing boats go down, search and rescue operations begin. Coast Guard and keepers work together to pull survivors to shore, salvage the wrecks and constantly monitor the area for other incidents.

I hope that my book brings to you, the reader, a sense of what lightkeeping today is all about. Here is one last image: at Estevan, the sweeping buttresses of the magnificent lighthouse, the most beautiful on the coast, stood between me and the blood-red sunset streaking the late spring sky. Gardens of sturdy, gem-like flowers spread at my feet. The rocky shore seemed to be lovingly stretched by the sea breezes for miles in both directions. My hair blew in the winds of the beautiful, cool evening. The clean scent of the ocean filled my lungs. But the reverie was broken by a conversation about the washed-in wreckage that had been seen down on the rocky beach, what boat the battered hull belonged to and when it might have gone down. Lightkeeping is a life of contrast, one of utter extremes.

Heart-Warming Soups
and Beverages

Point Atkinson

Lighthouse Borsch

Elaine and Donald Graham   *Point Atkinson*

Although the Grahams hardly fit into the "isolated lightkeeper" profile—
their children attend school in West Vancouver and Point Atkinson is close
to much of the best shopping in Canada—they were keepers for a number of
years at both Lucy and Bonilla Islands.

They are perhaps best known for their role in fighting the automation of
BC's lightstations and for Donald's two excellent histories of lightkeeping in
British Columbia, *Keepers of the Light* and *Lights of the Inside Passage*. Those
two volumes were my nightly reading aboard both the *George R. Pearkes* and
the *Martha L. Black*.

When they left Regina and headed for British Columbia, on their way to a
posting in Central America that never did materialize, they took with them
the recipes of Ukrainian prairie cooks. This soup recipe was "invaluable
during the winter months on lighthouses because root vegetables store so
well."

1 cup	thinly sliced carrots	250 mL
1 cup	diced celery	250 mL
2 cups	peeled, thinly sliced or grated raw beets	500 mL
2	medium onions, minced	2
6¾ cups	cold water or chicken stock (p. 13)	1675 mL
	salt and freshly ground pepper to taste	
3 tbsps	butter	45 mL
1 cup	shredded cabbage	250 mL
½ cup	sliced mushrooms, canned or fresh	125 mL
1 10 oz tin	tomato soup	1 284 mL tin
1 tbsp	lemon juice	15 mL
2 tbsps	all-purpose flour	25 mL
	sour cream as needed, for topping	

Combine the carrots, celery, beets and one minced onion in a large saucepan.
Pour in 6½ cups (1625 mL) of the water or stock and season to taste with
salt and pepper. Bring to a boil over medium heat, reduce the heat, cover and
simmer for 30 minutes.

Melt the butter in a skillet and gently sauté the remaining onion until
transparent. Toss in the cabbage and mushrooms; continue to cook for about
5 minutes, or until the vegetables are limp. Add to the borsch and cook until
the vegetables are tender.

Stir in the tomato soup and lemon juice. Taste and correct the seasonings
as necessary. Blend the flour with the water until smooth. Gently whisk into
the simmering borsch. Bring to a rapid boil and remove from the heat. Serve

in heated soup bowls and top with spoonfuls of sour cream or yogurt and sprinkle with dill.

Makes 6–8 servings.

Basic Chicken Stock

Elaine and Donald Graham   *Point Atkinson*

This stock can be made with an old stewing hen or from chicken parts that you have saved in the freezer. I always make a huge batch and freeze jars of it to be used in cooking everything from soups to rice.

3–4	cooking onions, minced	3–4
2–3	stalks celery plus leaves, chopped	2–3
1–2	diced carrots, peeled only if discoloured	1–2
1 tbsp	whole black peppercorns	15 mL
2–3	bay leaves	2–3
2 tsps	salt (optional)	10 mL
a handful	fresh or dried herbs that may suit your fancy, thyme, basil, marjoram, parsley...	a handful
1	large boiling fowl, about 6 lbs (2.5 kg)	1
	or	
	an assortment of chicken parts: backs, necks, wings, etc.	
	cold water, to cover	

Combine all ingredients in a large stock pot. Bring to a boil, cover and simmer for 4 or 5 hours. Skim periodically.

Strain the stock through a colander or cheesecloth-lined strainer. Chill and remove the fat that solidifies. Use immediately or reheat the gelled stock to pour into storage containers. Refrigerate for up to a week or freeze for up to 3 months.

Makes 3–4 quarts (3–4 L) depending on the amount of water you used.

"Back of the Stove" Vegetable Soup

Gwen and Doug Fraser   *Pine Island*

Gwen writes: "I have never used frozen veggies. I get fresh vegetables from my garden...broccoli, cauliflower and carrots. I don't measure, oh, I use about half a head of cauliflower, several carrots, and as far as broccoli goes, it must be cut up into between 1 and 2 cups. It's just one of those soups that get better in flavour the next day. I put it on in the morning, veggies and all, and just let it simmer all day."

1½ lbs	ground beef	680 g
1	medium onion, sliced	1
2 cups	stewed tomatoes	500 mL
7 cups	water	1.75 L
2	beef bouillon cubes	2
½ cup	long grain rice, uncooked	125 mL
2 tsps	salt	10 mL
½ tsp	basil	2 mL
¼ tsp	freshly ground pepper	1 mL
	loads of diced fresh vegetables	

In a 5 quart (5 L) Dutch oven brown the ground beef and the onion until all the pan juices evaporate. Drain any excess fat. Pour in the tomatoes and water. Toss in the bouillon, rice, salt, basil, pepper and vegetables. Cover and bring to a boil. Reduce the heat to low and simmer for as long as you want to, or until the vegetables are tender. Stir occasionally. Ladle into warmed soup bowls and serve with Gwen's Crusty Cheese Biscuits (p. 98).

Makes 8–10 servings.

Judy uses dark miso for stock. She adds several spoonfuls of it to water along with lots of vegetables and buckwheat noodles. She says that her soups are always leftovers and to increase their protein she ladles the steaming soup over chunks of cheese that she has divided among the soup bowls. (Judy Schweers, Ivory Island)

Clam Chowder

Wendy, Jim, Jessie and Melissa Abram   *Cape Mudge*

Wendy says that this is a great clam chowder for people who don't want to be reminded that they are eating clams... I guess it's possible to get sick of any wonderful thing, but fresh clams harvested just off the shore sound pretty good to me.

6 tbsps	butter	90 mL
1	large onion, chopped	1
1 cup	diced celery	250 mL
4 cups	diced, peeled potatoes (about 5 medium)	1 L

¼ cup	minced parsley	50 mL
½ tsp	salt	2 mL
¼ tsp	freshly ground pepper	1 mL
4 cups	chicken stock	1 L
5 strips	side bacon	5
5–6 tbsps	cornstarch	75–90 mL
½ cup	water	125 mL
3 cups	milk	750 mL
1–1½ cups	chopped cooked clams	250–325 mL
	or	
2 5 oz tins	baby clams, drained	2 142 g tins

Melt the butter in a large soup kettle. Add the onion and the celery, stirring over medium heat until transparent, about 10 minutes. Measure in the potatoes, parsley, salt, pepper and stock. Cover and bring to a boil. Reduce the heat and simmer until the potatoes are tender, about 30 minutes.

Meanwhile, cut the bacon into 1″ (2.5 cm) pieces and fry until crisp. Drain on paper towelling and add to the soup kettle.

Mix the cornstarch with the water and pour into the soup. Stir until thickened, 3 or 4 minutes. Add the milk and the clams. Gently reheat for 5–10 minutes, being careful not to allow it to boil. Taste and correct the seasonings. Serve with Gwen Fraser's Sunflower Seed Bread from Pine Island (p. 66) and you'll have a true taste of the Inside Passage.

Makes 8–10 steaming bowls.

Light Fish Chowder

Karen and John Coldwell   *McInnes Island*

Cougars are the terror of every mother on the lights. And when the Coldwells were keepers at Kains Island, on Vancouver Island's northwest coast, they had their first encounter with one. Karen had just put the baby out onto the front, fenced-in deck of their small clapboard house, and gone upstairs. When she glanced out the back window she saw the big cat skulking gracefully across the garden. She rushed downstairs to alert her husband and whisk the child to safety. By that time the cougar was well hidden in the prickly salmonberries that cascade over the front embankment down to the shore. Fortunately, it had to pop up to see where it was going and it was at that moment that John shot it. To my knowledge, no cougars have been sighted since at Kains.

This chowder goes back to the time when the children were babies. They loved it puréed, and as they grew up black bass became known as "chowder fish." Karen says that "black bass may be hard to clean, but are well worth the work for the taste they give the soup. Other fish can be used but somehow the bass is lighter and flakier."

¼ cup	butter	50 mL
1	medium onion, sliced	1
½ cup	sliced celery	125 mL
2 cups	boiling stock or water	500 mL
2 cups	diced potatoes	500 mL
½ cup	sliced carrots	125 mL
½ cup	fresh or frozen peas	125 mL
1 tsp	salt	5 mL
¼ tsp	freshly ground pepper	1 mL
½ tsp	seafood seasoning*	2 mL
1 lb	black bass fillets	450 g
2 cups	milk or half and half cream (10%)	500 mL

* I substituted a large pinch of thyme, a bit of basil and a shot of Tabasco sauce when I discovered that seafood seasoning is not always available here in Ontario.

Melt the butter in a heavy soup kettle or large saucepan. Toss in the onion and celery; sauté until tender, about 5–7 minutes. Add the stock, potatoes, carrots, peas, salt, pepper and seafood seasoning. Bring to a boil, cover and reduce the heat. Simmer for about 10 minutes or until the vegetables are cooked. Cut the fish into bite-sized pieces and stir into the soup. Simmer for another 10 minutes. Pour in the milk or cream and reheat without boiling. Taste and correct the seasonings. Ladle into heated soup bowls and serve with Karen's Not So Basic Bread (p. 73).

Makes 6–8 servings.

Orange Spiced Tea

Judy and Stan Westhaver   *Egg Island*

Tea is for the nose as much as it is for the palate. This one is particularly fragrant.

½ lb	orange pekoe tea	225 g
4 tsps	ground orange peel	20 mL
2	4″ (10 cm) cinnamon sticks	2
¼ cup	whole cloves	50 mL
¼ tsp	freshly grated nutmeg	1 mL
1 cup	slivered orange peel	250 mL

Quatsino

Combine the tea and ground orange peel. Crush the cinnamon sticks between two sheets of waxed paper and add to the tea along with the cloves and the nutmeg. When you are slivering the orange peel, be sure to remove as much of the pulp as possible. Stir into the tea mixture. Store in tightly covered glass containers.

Brew the tea as you normally would, about 1 tsp (5 mL) per serving.

Makes 4 cups (1 L) spiced tea mix.

Hot Spiced Apple Punch

Judy and Stan Westhaver   *Egg Island*

This recipe comes from the kitchen of Judy's mother-in-law's sister, Delena... how's that for a connection? It makes a huge batch of delicious non-alcoholic punch.

1 12 oz tin	frozen orange juice concentrate	1 341 mL tin
1 12 oz tin	frozen lemonade concentrate	1 341 mL tin
2 12 oz tins	frozen apple juice concentrate	2 341 mL tins
1 cup	granulated sugar	250 mL
2	cinnamon sticks	2
10	whole cloves	10
½ tsp	ground ginger	2 mL
½ tsp	ground allspice	2 mL
5 quarts	cold water	5 L

Put the juice concentrates into a large preserving kettle. Stir in the sugar and spices. Pour in the cold water, a quart at a time, stirring to dissolve the sugar. Place over medium heat and bring to a simmer for 15–20 minutes until spicy and steaming.

Makes 35 servings.

Tangy Salads and Dressings, and Some Unusual Vegetables

Langara Point

Pacific Northwest Salad

Judy, Gorden and Guthrie Schweers — *Ivory Island*

In Seattle, just before I boarded the *Martha L. Black*, I attended a conference on Pacific Northwest Cookery. It was filled with some of the most knowledgeable food people in the west. If any one trait is characteristic of PNW foods, it is the immediacy with which they are prepared: fresh from the garden or the sea to the table.

The salad that Judy shared with me on that cold, drizzling Pacific day could be considered quintessential! Leafy Swiss chard and turnip greens, a handful of fresh basil, cucumbers and cherry tomatoes from their stone-walled greenhouse. The dressing was the following one, strong enough to complement the winter greens...it was truly delicious!

I suggest that you double or triple this recipe because it really improves with age.

¼ cup	olive oil	50 mL
2 tsps	rice wine vinegar or cider vinegar	10 mL
1	garlic clove, minced	1
	or	
¼ tsp	garlic powder	1 mL
¼ tsp	salt	1 mL
¼ tsp	dry mustard	1 mL
⅛ tsp	freshly ground pepper	.5 mL

Whisk all the ingredients together and pour into a glass decanter or small jar. Cover and let stand for a few hours or overnight before serving.

Makes about ½ cup (125 mL).

The Nootka Story

Before taking over Ivory Island, the Schweerses were posted at Nootka, a beautiful station surrounded by wild flowers and great fishing. It was at Nootka that they purchased their dependable wood/airtight stove that figures in this story and in their entire way of life from then on.

In April or May of 1981, nineteen canoeists set out for a jaunt, against the advice of the weatherman. The leader was an experienced guide, but didn't realize that a strong south-wester was on the way. When they attempted to return, the drift of the water and the push of the wind drove them into the rocks, smashing canoes and scattering the canoeists along the shoreline. They were about six miles from the Nootka lightstation, which was their only hope. Men and women hiked in cold, wet, hypothermic groups and finally reached the Schweers family.

The weather was still howling when they arrived with one man missing. Judy "cranked the stove up as high as it'd go." It was like a sauna with drying clothes and soggy people. Immediately she threw a whole salmon (one that she and Gorden had caught) into the almost molten oven of the woodstove, put a big pot of herbed rice on the top and defrosted five or six loaves of her own wonderful wholewheat bread. She provided a huge salad of winter greens and within a couple of hours all twenty-one of them were eating a meal fit for royalty. There were no injuries, except perhaps the pride of the guide. As an added bonus, a Japanese lady who was part of the ill-fated expedition invited Judy and Gorden to visit her, and when they did she toured them all around Japan.

Make Ahead Cabbage Slaw

Judy and Stan Westhaver   *Egg Island*

Judy makes huge batches of this salad during barbecue season so there is "always a batch on the go and always a batch ready."

Egg Island yields many of their fresh vegetables and fruits—perfect for Stan's other main pastime, wine-making. As I sat waiting for the Sikorski to fly me to Pointer Island, Stan explained that "On Egg Island, if it moves, we turn it into wine." By the time the big chopper finally landed, we had sampled the beet, turnip and carrot vintages of the past few years, giggling and praying each time a new bottle was opened that the helicopter would be late. Stan wrapped several bottles of carrot wine (the best was the 1985 vintage) for Captain Mellis aboard the *Black*. He was instructed to share it...he didn't!

1	large green cabbage	1
3	carrots	3
1	large cooking onion	1
1	red pepper	1
1	green pepper	1
1 cup	diced celery	250 mL
1 cup	granulated sugar	250 mL
1 cup	vegetable oil	250 mL
1 cup	white vinegar	250 mL
1 tsp	prepared mustard (I prefer Dijon)	5 mL
1 tsp	celery seeds	5 mL

Grate the cabbage and the carrots. Slice the onion thinly. Cut the tops off the red and green peppers; chop finely, including the seeds. Put all the vegetables into a large mixing bowl.

In a saucepan, combine the sugar, oil, vinegar, mustard and celery seeds. Bring to a boil, reduce the heat and simmer for 5 minutes. Pour over the vegetables, stirring to coat evenly. Store in a covered jar or a crock for up to 4 weeks.

Makes about 2–4 quarts (2–4 L) depending on the size of the cabbage.

Everlasting Coleslaw

Darlene, Allan, Walter and Athena Tansky   *Scarlett Point*

Surrounded by a high picket fence to keep the deer from munching, the Scarlett Point garden holds all sorts of herbs and vegetables, from sassafras for tea and salads, to mint, lettuces and spaghetti squash.

1	large cabbage	1
1	large onion	1
4	carrots	4
½ cup	brown sugar	125 mL
½ cup	white vinegar	125 mL
½ cup	vegetable oil	125 mL
1 tsp	dry mustard	5 mL

Shred the cabbage, onion and carrots. Toss together in a large bowl. Heat the sugar, vinegar, oil and mustard together in a small saucepan. Bring to a boil, remove from the heat and cool. Pour over the prepared vegetables. Transfer to a glass or other non-corrosive container. Cover and chill in the refrigerator for up to two weeks.

Makes 3–4 quarts (3–4 L).

Marinated Onion Salad

Judy and Stan Westhaver   *Egg Island*

Judy still laughs when she tells this story: a member of one of the work crews was very, very hungry after a long day. He innocently thought that this dish was pasta in a cream sauce (they do look alike) and shovelled a huge pile onto his plate, only to find out that what he had was a dish full of onions.

This is a good side dish, but I especially like it on grilled hamburgers. Now if only I had some of Stan's famous carrot wine to wash it all down...

4	large mild onions	4
1 cup	white vinegar	250 mL
1 cup	granulated sugar	250 mL
1 cup	mayonnaise (below)	250 mL
1 tbsps	celery salt	15 mL

Slice the onions into ¼" (5 mm) rings. Bring the vinegar and sugar to a boil in a saucepan. Pour over the onion slices and marinate in a covered container for 8 hours or overnight. Drain off the liquid and squeeze out as much moisture as possible. Toss with the mayonnaise and celery salt. Chill before serving.

Makes 4–6 servings.

Blender Mayonnaise

Judy, Gorden and Guthrie Schweers   *Ivory Island*

This is an almost instant version of the classic recipe. If you use apple cider vinegar, the mayonnaise is mild enough to slather on homemade bread or crackers and top with your favourite smoked fish. Rae Gamble (another lover of good food) and I sat at our kitchen table one winter's night with a chunk of smoked Georgian Bay splake, a crunchy loaf of Quatsino Wholewheat Bread (p. 71), a little butter, this mayonnaise and some Kelp Pickles (p. 32), washing it all down with a bottle of full-bodied red wine...recipe testing is so difficult.

2	eggs, at room temperature	2
¼ cup	apple cider vinegar	50 mL
¼ tsp	salt	1 mL
½–1 tsp	dry mustard	2–5 mL
1½ cups	vegetable oil	375 mL

Place all ingredients except the oil into a blender or food processor. Process until smooth. With the machine still running, pour in the oil in a steady stream. Blend well. Store in a glass jar in the refrigerator.

Makes about 2 cups (500 mL).

Golden Chanterelles

Vivian and Bob Bodnar   *Scarlett Point*

British Columbia has the very best wild mushrooms in all of Canada. Vivian and Bob are veteran stalkers of the chanterelles that grow in their secret spot. "Every fall, Bob and I load the aluminum skiff with cardboard boxes and head to our favourite location. We pick mushrooms up the hill and have lunch on top, about 100 feet above sea level. Then we pick our way down, load the boat and head home. It takes about four days to put away all the mushrooms I need for a year."

Vivian prefers to dry them rather than can them. She feels that it is just too difficult to clean them well enough to can them safely. She uses a food drier or simply the oven.

Drying Chanterelles

Clean the mushrooms, using a minimum of water. Cut them into slices about ¼" (6 mm) thick and spread evenly over a clean screen. Put the screen on top of the oven rack and turn the heat to as low a setting as your oven has. Prop the door open to allow the moist air to escape. When the chanterelles are dry, they will feel tough and leather-like. Store in tightly closed containers. Vivian recommends a coffee tin with a plastic lid.

Using Dried Mushrooms

If they were well cleaned before drying, they may simply be dropped, as is, into simmering spaghetti sauce, soups or stews. Vivian says that they will add flavour but will remain a little chewy.

To reconstitute them, add the dried chanterelles to a small amount of boiling water, continuing to boil for about a minute. Remove from the heat and let stand for 15–30 minutes to allow any sediment to settle. Remove the mushrooms with a slotted spoon and strain the remaining liquid. The mushroom "water" is an excellent addition to soups, gravies or sauces.

Freezing Chanterelles

Clean, slice and sauté the chanterelles in a little butter. Add minced garlic, a few drops of olive oil, oregano, catnip or parsley. Freeze in well-sealed containers. Vivian says that this base can be used for gravy or soup, or just heated and served as is. To make a mushroom paste, simply puree in a food processor or food mill and freeze in small batches. Spread a small amount of the pungent paste on roast beef or steak.

Chanterelle Soufflé

Vivian and Bob Bodnar   *Scarlett Point*

⅓ cup	butter	75 mL
2 cups	chopped fresh chanterelles	500 mL
4	green onions, sliced	4
1	garlic clove, crushed	1
¼ cup	all-purpose flour	50 mL

1 cup	milk	250 mL
2 tbsps	dry sherry or white wine	25 mL
½ cup	grated cheese: cheddar, brick, Monterey Jack...whatever	125 mL
½ tsp	salt	2 mL
¼ tsp	freshly ground pepper	1 mL
	cayenne pepper to taste	
4	eggs, separated, at room temperature	4

Preheat the oven to 350°F (180°C).

Melt 2 tbsps (25 mL) of the butter in a skillet and sauté the mushrooms, green onions and garlic until all the liquid has evaporated. Remove with a slotted spoon and set aside.

Melt the remaining butter in the skillet and stir in the flour. Cook gently for several minutes. Whisk in the milk and allow the mixture to thicken. Add the sherry, cheese, salt, pepper and cayenne. Remove from the heat.

Beat the egg yolks in a separate bowl. Pour a little of the hot mixture into the bowl, beating constantly. Pour the egg mixture into the skillet. Add the reserved mushroom mixture.

In a separate bowl, beat the egg whites until stiff and fold in gently to the soufflé base. Pour into an ungreased 1 quart (1 L) soufflé dish and set into a pan with 1" (2.5 cm) hot water. Bake for 45–50 minutes or until the edges are puffed and browning. Serve immediately.

Makes 4 servings.

Creamed Chicken of the Woods

Lise, Ken and Noah Brunn   *Langara Point*

Chicken of the Woods (*Polyporus sulfureus*) is a shelf fungus that is unmistakable to even the amateur mycologist. Its orangish lobes are found clustered on rotting logs and even on living trees. Lise says that it's best to use only the tender edges of the fungus for this dish...I'll have to take her word for it because I haven't been able to find any here in southern Ontario, or even when I was on a mycological expedition near Sooke, BC.

1 lb	tender edges of the Chicken of the Woods fungus	450 g
2–3 tbsps	butter	25–45 mL
2	small leeks, washed and thinly sliced	2
1 tbsp	all-purpose flour	15 mL
1 cup	table cream (18%) or evaporated milk	250 mL
	salt and freshly ground pepper	

Ballenas Island

Wash and trim the fungus if needed. Slice thinly. Melt the butter in a skillet and add the Chicken of the Woods. Toss in the sliced leeks and sauté very slowly for 15–20 minutes over low heat or until the butter is absorbed and the vegetables are tender. Sprinkle with the flour and stir in the cream. Simmer for a few minutes until thickened. Season to taste with salt and pepper.

Makes 4 servings.

Mushrooms in Soy Sauce

Gwen and Doug Fraser   *Pine Island*

Pine Island is the nesting ground for a species of rare Canadian bird: the Rhinocerous Billed Auklet. I'm not kidding, that's the name. According to Doug, they are sea-oriented birds that come ashore to burrow and nest. Unfortunately, they are not used to such minor details as trees that get in their way, so many of them crash and die. At that point the Frasers gather the small bodies and ship them to the provincial museum in Victoria. The Canadian Wildlife Federation periodically goes to Pine Island to band them, carefully digging up the chicks from the small holes in the spongy forest soil.

Try this delicious way of cooking mushrooms—it will work beautifully with the wild varieties as well.

2–3 cups	fresh mushrooms	500–750 mL
1 tbsp	all-purpose flour	15 mL
3 tbsps	butter	45 mL
1 tsp	soy sauce	5 mL

Wash the mushrooms and drain well. Leave whole or slice. Toss gently with the flour. Heat the butter and soy sauce in a skillet. Sauté the mushrooms over low heat for 8–10 minutes, turning occasionally.

Makes 4 servings.

Myriad Spaghetti Squash Dishes

Vivian and Bob Bodnar   *Scarlett Point*

Vivian grows as many spaghetti squash as she can because they keep so well over the winter in her cool, dry basement.

Basic Preparation

Cut each squash in half and remove the seeds, which can be saved for planting next spring. Place the squash in a pan with 1″ (2.5 cm) water. Cover tightly with foil and bake in a 400°F (200°C) oven until the squash releases its spaghetti-like strands. It will take between 45 minutes and 1 hour depending on the size of the vegetable. It may also be cooked in the microwave on High for about 10 minutes per half. Cover with plastic wrap instead of foil and add only a few spoonfuls of water.

When it is cooked, remove the spaghetti strands with a fork, combining them with any of the following fillings. Pile the stuffing back into the shell and warm thoroughly before serving.

Apple Stuffing

Serve as a side dish with ham, pork or sausage.

1	medium spaghetti squash, cooked	1
½ cup	brown sugar	125 mL
¼ cup	melted butter	50 mL
2	apples, cored and thinly sliced	2

Preheat the oven to 350°F (180°C).

Toss the squash with the sugar, butter and apples. Mound into the squash shell, cover with foil and bake for 20 minutes or until heated through and steaming.

Sour Cream Stuffing

1	medium spaghetti squash, cooked	1
1 cup	sour cream	250 ml
1	small onion, minced	1
½ tsp	salt	2 mL
¼ tsp	freshly ground pepper	1 mL
	buttered crumbs, as needed	

Preheat the oven to 350°F (180°C).

Combine the sour cream and the spaghetti squash. Stir in the onion, salt and pepper. Pile into the squash shells. Top with buttered crumbs. Place on a cookie sheet and bake until the topping begins to brown.

Spaghetti Squash with Sausage Stuffing

Vivian and Bob Bodnar   *Scarlett Point*

We like to use a spicy sausage like Chorizo in this recipe. But any other farm-style sausage would suffice.

1	large spaghetti squash	1
1½ lbs	sausage	575 g
¾ cup	chopped onion	175 mL
½ cup	diced red pepper	125 mL
½ tsp	garlic powder	2 mL
2 tsps	dried oregano	10 mL
1/2 tsp	freshly ground pepper	2 mL
1½ cups	shredded mozzarella cheese	375 mL

Wash the squash and cut it in half. Cook as directed on p. 27. With a fork, pull the cooked strands into a large mixing bowl.

Preheat the oven to 350°F (180°C).

Remove the sausage meat from its casings and fry in a skillet until well cooked and thoroughly browned. Drain off any excess fat. Toss in the onion and red pepper. Season with the garlic powder, oregano and freshly ground pepper. Cook, stirring, for 5 minutes or until the onion is transparent. Add to the spaghetti squash in the mixing bowl. Combine thoroughly. Pile back into the squash shells and place on a baking sheet. Top with the cheese and bake for 25–35 minutes or until the cheese is melted and bubbling. Serve immediately with a green salad and a loaf of Stan's Compost Bread (p. 74).

Makes 6–8 generous servings.

Vegetables au Gratin

Linda and Don Weeden   *Cape Scott*

When Linda needs a recipe to perk up those rapidly fading winter vegetables, this is it.

¼ cup	mayonnaise (p. 23)	50 mL
2 tbsps	all-purpose flour	25 mL
1 cup	milk	250 mL
½ tsp	salt	2 mL
¼ tsp	freshly ground pepper	1 mL
½ tsp	Italian seasoning or a mixture of basil and oregano	2 mL
¼ cup	minced onion	50 mL
4–6 cups	sliced vegetables, such as carrots, zucchini or green beans, lightly steamed	1.5 L
½ cup	fresh bread crumbs	125 mL
¼ cup	grated Parmesan cheese	50 mL
2 tbsps	melted butter	25 mL

Whisk the mayonnaise, flour and milk together. Season with salt and pepper. Add the seasonings and the onion. Place over medium heat and cook, stirring constantly, until thickened.

Butter a 1½ quart (1.5 L) casserole and fill with vegetables. Cover with the sauce.

Combine the bread crumbs, cheese and melted butter. Spread over the casserole. Place under the broiler for 4–6 minutes or until golden and bubbling.

Makes 4–6 servings.

Waldorf Rice

Lee Wehrwein-Gilbert and John Gilbert, Matthew, Sasha and Oban   *Ballenas Island*

The Junior Keeper's house where Lee, John and their children live is nestled in the rock face of the island. An old bent apple tree droops over the house, and otters play on the shore where the family gather sea vegetables for drying. Lee and John live life to its fullest, and stick to a macrobiotic diet. This lifestyle has its advantages for people on the lights: dried lentils and legumes can easily be stored for months. Lee and John make their own tofu, a vegetarian staple.

This recipe was designed for a pressure cooker, but if you cover the rice tightly when cooking over low heat, it will be perfect after about an hour. It goes particularly well with Halibut in Engevita Sauce (p. 40).

2 cups	brown rice, preferably long grain	500 mL
⅛ tsp	sea salt	.5 mL
3 cups	stock or water	750 mL
½ cup	diagonally sliced celery	125 mL
¼ cup	raisins	50 mL
½ cup	roasted chopped walnuts	125 mL

Combine the rice, salt and stock in a pressure cooker. Stir in the celery, raisins and walnuts. Cover and bring to pressure slowly, cooking on low heat for 45 minutes. Fluff with a fork before serving.

Makes 4–6 servings.

Try this super condiment on freshly steamed rice or vegetables. Rinse 1 cup (250 mL) sesame seeds and roast them until golden brown in a dry skillet. I use my reliable old cast iron frying pan. Grind them either with a mortar and pestle or in a food processor. Lee uses a Japanese suribachi (serrated clay bowl) with a surikogi (wooden pestle). Add 2½ tbsps (35 mL) sea salt and 1 tbsp (15 mL) kelp powder, which may be found in most whole food stores. Grind together briefly before storing in a tightly covered container. It does not require refrigeration. (Lee Wehrwein-Gilbert, Ballenas Island)

Crunchy Pickles, Relishes, and Other Preserves

Estevan Point

Kelp Pickles

Vivian and Bob Bodnar *Scarlett Point*

After my voyage on the *Martha L. Black*, I flew home full of nostalgia and longing to return to the sea. In my mail, among the bills and the junk littering the dining room table, there was a large package awaiting me. It was postmarked Port Hardy and was tightly bundled in layers of packing tape and styrofoam. Bits of parcel flew until I reached the contents. Vivian had harvested the kelp and pickled it, and knowing that I would probably never have the opportunity to taste such pickles again, had sent all three kinds. For a foodie like me, there could be no better gift.

In her package, she also included the following recipes and commentary about kelp. Vivian writes: "The bladder kelp *(Nereocystis luetkeanan)* grows in salt water. Firmly attached to a submerged rock, a long stalk leads up to a bulbous float on the surface of the water. Four groups of broad, flat blades grow like long ears from the top of the float. This kelp is thick and strong.

"Kelp beds mark submerged rocks which is an assist to boaters. Kelp is an annual plant and can grow to 20 meters long with a float over 12 inches in diameter. There is enough carbon monoxide in the float to kill a chicken.

"In the fall we harvest this kelp to mulch the garden. In the spring, I harvest it for pickles.

"To collect kelp one needs a small boat and calm seas. I take along a butcher knife and a potato scraper. Half meter sections of kelp are cut and the outer skin is peeled off with a potato scraper as one would pare a carrot.

"In the kitchen these stem pieces are put through a food processor resulting in large rings of varying sizes. The rings are put into a large bowl and covered with fresh water. For the next four days or so, the water is changed frequently until the kelp is 'freshened.' When freshened, the rings will have a neutral taste, the water will be clear and the rings will feel dry rather than slimy.

"Kelp is nice because it retains a crunch. The coastal Indians have always used kelp both for eating and as storage containers. They used to store eulachon grease in the bulb and the stalk, coil it and keep it in cedar boxes."

Sweet Pickled Kelp

Vivian and Bob Bodnar *Scarlett Point*

This recipe should begin: "First you take a good rowboat..."

4 cups	freshened kelp rings (see above for method)	1 L
2 cups	granulated sugar	500 mL

| 2 cups | white vinegar | 500 mL |
| 2 tbsps | mixed whole pickling spice, tied in a cheesecloth bag | 25 mL |

Measure the kelp rings by packing them tightly. Bring the sugar and vinegar to a boil in a heavy saucepan. Drop in the spices and allow the syrup to simmer for 10 minutes. Pour the boiling syrup over the kelp rings, cover and allow it to stand overnight. Repeat this procedure each day for the next 3 days.

On the fourth day, drain off the liquid and bring to a boil. Add the rings and return the mixture to a boil. Discard the spice bag. Pack the rings into hot sterilized jars, pouring the boiling syrup over them. Run a sterilized spoon around the pickles to release any air bubbles. Wipe off any syrup from around the jar edges. Seal and store in a cool, dark place.

Makes two 16 oz (500 mL) jars.

Dilled Kelp Rings

Vivian and Bob Bodnar   *Scarlett Point*

½ cup	coarse pickling salt	125 mL
3 cups	white vinegar	750 mL
3 cups	water	750 mL
14 cups	freshened kelp rings (see method p. 32)	3.5 L
16	garlic cloves	16
4 tsps	whole mustard seed	20 mL
	dill heads or dill seed, as needed	

Bring the salt, vinegar and water to a boil in a large non-metallic saucepan. Reduce the heat and let simmer for 5 minutes. Add the kelp rings and return to a boil. Immediately remove from the heat.

Pack each of 8 sterilized pint (16 oz/500 mL) jars with 2 cloves of garlic, ½ tsp mustard seed and at least 2 dill heads or 1½ tbsps (20 mL) dried or fresh dill seed. Add the kelp rings and hot brine. Release any air bubbles by running a sterilized spoon around the pickles. Seal the jars. Store in a cool, dark place for at least 6 weeks for the flavour to develop.

Makes eight 16 oz (500 mL) jars.

Zucchini Relish

Gwen and Doug Fraser   *Pine Island*

The rich, woodsy soil full of organic material is perfect for growing a whole variety of vegetables. Gwen says that zucchini grow in profusion.

12 cups	coarsely ground zucchini, unpeeled	4 L
2	ground green peppers	2
2	chopped red peppers	2
4 cups	coarsely ground onions	1 L
⅓ cup	pickling salt	75 mL
1 tsp	turmeric	5 mL
1 tsp	curry powder	5 mL
1 tsp	celery seed	5 mL
1 tbsp	cornstarch	15 mL
½ tsp	freshly ground pepper	2 mL
4½ cups	granulated sugar	1.125 L
3 cups	white vinegar	750 mL

Combine the zucchini, peppers and onions in a large non-metallic mixing bowl. Sprinkle with the pickling salt and let stand overnight. In the morning, drain thoroughly. Rinse with cold water. Drain well a second time and transfer to a large saucepan that has a heavy bottom. Mix the turmeric, curry powder, celery seed, cornstarch, pepper and sugar. Whisk in the vinegar. Add to the vegetable mixture. Cook, stirring constantly, over medium heat until the relish begins to boil. Reduce the heat and simmer for 20 minutes, still stirring. Pour into sterilized jars and seal. Store in a cool, dark place.

Makes six 16 oz (500 mL) jars.

Cucumber Relish

Pauline, Joe and Cindy Balmer   *Estevan Point*

Pauline uses other vegetables like carrots or beans in this recipe to "clean up the garden at the end of the season." Not only is this relish reasonably quick and easy, it's delicious!

4 cups	chopped, unpeeled cucumbers	1 L
4 cups	chopped, unpeeled green tomatoes	1 L
2 cups	chopped onions	500 mL
1	small green cabbage	1
2	red peppers, seeded	2

2	green peppers, seeded	2
½ cup	pickling salt	125 mL
	hot water, as needed	
¼ cup	dry mustard	50 mL
2 tbsps	turmeric	25 mL
4 cups	granulated sugar	1 L
4 cups	white vinegar	1 L

Put all the vegetables through a food chopper or grinder, pouring them into a large non-metallic bowl as you are chopping them. Sprinkle with the pickling salt and cover with hot water. Let stand for 30 minutes, then drain thoroughly.

Combine the mustard, turmeric, sugar and vinegar in a large, heavy saucepan. Bring to a boil and stir in the drained vegetables. Return to a boil and cook, stirring often to prevent sticking, for 30 minutes. Ladle into sterilized jars and seal.

Makes seven or eight 16 oz (500 mL) jars.

Bread and Butter Pickles

Pauline, Joe and Cindy Balmer   *Estevan Point*

Pauline says that zucchini works as well as cucumbers in this recipe.

16 cups	sliced, unpeeled cucumbers	4 L
6	medium onions, peeled and sliced	6
2	green peppers, seeded and sliced	2
3	garlic cloves, minced	3
⅓ cup	pickling salt	75 mL
	crushed ice, as needed	
5 cups	granulated sugar	1.25 L
3 cups	apple cider vinegar	750 mL
1½ tsps	turmeric	7 mL
1½ tsps	celery seed	7 mL
2 tbsps	mustard seed	25 mL

Place the prepared vegetables in a large non-metallic bowl. Sprinkle with the salt and then cover with a layer of crushed ice. Let stand for 3 hours; drain thoroughly.

In a large saucepan, combine the sugar, vinegar, turmeric, celery seed and mustard seed. Add the well-drained vegetables and bring to a boil over medium high heat. Ladle into sterilized jars and seal. Store in a cool, dark place.

Makes eight to nine 16 oz (500 mL) jars.

Pine Island

Jalapeño Pepper Jelly

Judy and Stan Westhaver   *Egg Island*

The Westhavers grow their own cayenne and jalapeño peppers in their greenhouse. This jelly is great with cream cheese on thinly sliced Miso Bread (p. 75) or as a condiment with sausage or pork chops.

10–14	jalapeño peppers	10–14
6½ cups	granulated sugar	1.625 L
1½ cups	apple cider vinegar	375 mL
1 6 oz bottle	liquid pectin	1 170 mL bottle

Wear rubber gloves when handling hot peppers. Wash the peppers, remove the seeds and the membrane. Pulse in either a food processor or a blender, using the on and off switch to chop coarsely. Pour into a large, heavy saucepan along with the sugar and vinegar. Bring to a boil, stirring constantly. Boil hard for 1 minute. Remove from the heat and cool for 5 minutes. Thoroughly stir in the pectin. Ladle into sterilized jars and seal. Store in a cool, dark place.

   Makes six or seven 8 oz (500 mL) jars.

Green Tomato Mincemeat

Judy and Stan Westhaver   *Egg Island*

There are always green tomatoes left at the end of the short northern growing season. I'm surprised that Stan hasn't tried making wine with them, or perhaps we just didn't get to that shelf in his wine cellar.

10 cups	prepared green tomatoes (see below)	2.5 L
	cold water, as needed	
6 cups	brown sugar, lightly packed	1.5 L
4 cups	raisins	1 L
2 cups	chopped candied mixed peel or citron peel	500 mL
½ cup	shortening or butter	125 mL
⅔ cup	cider vinegar	150 mL
4 tsps	salt	20 mL
2 tsps	cinnamon	10 ml
1 tsp	freshly grated nutmeg	5 mL
1 tsp	ground cloves	5 mL
⅔ cup	unsweetened grape juice	150 mL

To prepare the tomatoes, wash them and cut off the stems. Slice them into quarters and put through a food chopper, using a coarse blade, until you have 10 cups (2.5 L). Drain excess liquid and place tomatoes in a large kettle. Cover with cold water and bring to a boil. Remove from the heat and let stand for 30 minutes. Drain well. Stir in the brown sugar, raisins, peel, shortening, vinegar, salt and spices. Cook over medium heat, stirring often, until thickened. Pour in the grape juice and return to a boil. Boil for 2 minutes. Pour into sterilized jars and process in a pressure canner at 10 lbs pressure for 25 minutes. Or pack into plastic containers and freeze. The mincemeat may be stored in the refrigerator in tightly sealed containers for 2–3 weeks.

Makes about 10 cups (2.5 L) or enough for 2 large pies plus a dozen tarts.

Mincemeat Pie

Use 4 cups of mincemeat for every 9″ (22 cm) unbaked pie shell. Spread evenly, top with either a crust or lattice pastry strips and bake in a preheated 425°F (220°C) oven for 10 minutes. Reduce the heat to 350°F (180°C) and continue to bake until the pastry is golden and the filling is bubbly, about 25 minutes.

Rhubarb Ginger Jam

Judy and Stan Westhaver   *Egg Island*

Rhubarb grows well in the cool maritime climate that is common to the northern BC coast. Stan uses it to make his wine and Judy stirs up batches of this aromatic jam.

4 cups	thinly sliced rhubarb	1 L
¼ cup	syrup from preserved ginger	50 mL
½	cup water	125 mL
5¼ cups	granulated sugar	1.3 L
½ cup	finely chopped preserved ginger	125 mL
½ bottle	liquid pectin	½ bottle

Combine the rhubarb, ginger syrup and water in a large saucepan. Cover and bring to a boil. Reduce the heat and simmer until the rhubarb is tender, about 1–2 minutes. Stir in the sugar and preserved ginger. Bring to a full rolling boil, stirring constantly. Boil hard, still stirring, for 1 minute. Remove from the heat and pour in the pectin. Stir and skim for 5 minutes. Ladle into sterilized jars and seal. Store in a dark, cool place...there are lots of those on the lightstations.

Makes six 8 oz (250 mL) jars.

Fish, Shellfish, Meat, Game and a Few Vegetarian Dishes

Entrance Island

Halibut in Engevita Cream Sauce

Judy, Gorden and Guthrie Schweers   *Ivory Island*

The halibut was caught by Judy and Gorden in their little boat just off the shore at Ivory. There was a tremendous tug on their line and as they pulled the struggling fish into the boat, wee Guthrie ducked and hid under the seat — he had never seen a sixty-pound fish before.

In their kitchen, warmed by a wonderful old woodstove and enveloped by the aroma of baking cinnamon buns, we ate this halibut, with what I would call a true Pacific Northwest Salad (p. 20). It was a light, satisfying meal. Afterwards, we all grabbed a cinnamon bun, and with Guthrie holding tightly onto both our hands, Judy and I swung along the mossy, slippery boardwalk down to their favourite cove where the herring spawn. Through the rain forest, fern and moss-covered branches hanging overhead, we talked about Judy's philosophy of eating. She and I agree that freshest is best and that we all have to become much more aware of the resources around us. These are very old-fashioned values: harvesting the land was once the only means of survival. Now it is possible to buy raspberries in December, but somehow the very essence of the food is lost. The seasonality brings with it a joy and satisfaction that no marketing strategist can replace.

Judy and Gorden harvest the sea. They not only fish for cod, salmon and halibut, but they gather abalone, scallops, octopus (which is not Guthrie's favourite meal), and red spiny sea urchins. Judy is becoming very knowledgeable about the use of sea vegetables. For help and guidance, she turns to Larry Golden, the keeper at Triple Island north of Prince Rupert, who is a sea vegetable expert. He studies them professionally and has discovered at least one new variety.

When we arrived at the cove, Judy told me the story of Kwathmus — a salty seaweed delicacy that is very rare. At about the end of February, the herring come here to spawn. They rush into quiet bays and reproduce furiously, coating the young kelp fronds with creamy, bubbly foam. The coastal Indians traditionally harvested the narrow kelp and dried it beside their campfires. The crispy results were relished as one of the first true tastes of spring. Judy, being an adopted member of an Indian family at Bella Bella, also harvests the Kwathmus and when I arrived back in Ontario there was a big package of it waiting for me.

The following recipe may be adapted for any kind of fish. If you use frozen fillets, make a slightly thicker sauce by increasing the amount of flour by 1 tbsp (15 mL). Purchase the engevita yeast at any health food store.

| ¼ cup | butter or vegetable oil | 50 mL |
| 3 tbsps | wholewheat flour | 45 mL |

3 tbsps	engevita yeast	45 mL
2 cups	milk or stock	500 mL
¼ tsp	cayenne pepper	2 mL
1 cup	grated edam, gouda or havarti cheese	250 mL
2 lbs	halibut fillets (6–8), approx. 3/4″ (2 cm) thick	900 g
	paprika, as needed	

Preheat the oven to 350°F (180°C).

In a medium saucepan melt the butter. Stir in the flour and yeast, cooking over low heat until bubbly and slightly browned. Slowly whisk in the milk and continue to simmer until thickened. Season with cayenne. Remove from the heat and stir in the cheese.

Lay the fish fillets in an oiled baking dish. I used a 9″ x 13″ (3.5 L) rectangular pan. Pour the sauce evenly over the fish and sprinkle with a light dusting of paprika. Bake, uncovered, for 45 minutes or until the top is golden brown. Judy cautions that this time may vary depending on the thickness of the fillets.

Makes 6–8 servings.

Baked Marinated Salmon

Kathy Heise and Lance Barrett-Lennard   *Boat Bluff*

Climbing up the steep banks at low tide towards the station, I wasn't really sure what my reception would be. I had received a long letter from Kathy just before I left Ontario stating that neither she nor Lance was a very good cook and almost apologizing for being nearly vegetarian. What I found was a couple who are indeed more interested in studying killer whales than in cooking, but who are also quite committed to excellent, if simple, meals.

"Keep in mind," Kathy wrote, "that our favourite dinner is brown rice topped with engevita yeast and soy sauce with some veggies on the side." But this salmon dish, a recipe that appears in many variations up and down the coast, was so good that when I tested it on my boys, I had to act as referee at the table.

1½ lbs	salmon fillet	680 g
2 tbsps	brown sugar	25 mL
½ tsp	garlic powder	2 mL
3 tbsps	soy sauce	45 mL
1 tbsp	lemon juice	15 mL

Lay the salmon fillets in a baking dish and spread evenly with brown sugar.

Sprinkle with garlic powder, soy sauce and lemon juice. Cover tightly with plastic wrap, refrigerate and allow to marinate for up to 8 hours. As Kathy says, it will turn a darkish brown and smell delicious even before it's cooked.

Preheat the oven to 350°F (180°C) or 400°F (200°C) if, as Kathy comments, "you aren't overcome by the heat of the oil stove!"

Bake, uncovered, for about 15 minutes at 350°F (180°C) or for 10–12 minutes if your oven is set at 400°F (200°C). Baste occasionally with the juices that accumulate in the pan.

This salmon is also excellent barbecued over medium coals.

Makes 6–8 servings.

The hardest part of canning salmon is catching the fish. Judy and Gorden Schweers use a handliner to do all their fishing. As Judy describes it, it is a little 8–9″ stick wrapped with line and connected to a weight, a flasher and a lure. They use this method to catch cod, halibut, salmon and various kinds of Pacific rockfish. They even caught an octopus which provided them with five meals.

After catching and cleaning the salmon, they simply slice it up into mason jars, without adding any salt or oil. They seal the jars and process them for 90 minutes at 15 lbs pressure. Any scraps are canned for pet food. (Judy Schweers, Ivory Island)

Basic Salmon Loaf

Judy and Stan Westhaver   *Egg Island*

This is almost like the salmon loaf that I loved as a child. I remember cutting slabs off the cold loaf and eating them with homemade pickles after school.

⅓ cup	milk	75 mL
⅔ cup	crushed soda crackers	150 mL
1 tbsp	minced fresh parsley	15 mL
1 tbsp	minced green onions or chives	15 mL
1 tsp	salt (omit if you use salted crackers)	5 mL
1 tbsp	lemon juice	15 mL
2	eggs, beaten	2
2 cups	canned salmon, flaked	500 mL

Preheat the oven to 350°F (180°C).

Combine the milk and crackers in a small saucepan. Heat to boiling, reduce the heat and simmer for 2–3 minutes. Stir in the parsley, onions, salt, lemon juice, eggs and salmon. Mix thoroughly and press into a well-greased 4½″

x 8½" (1.5 L) loaf pan. Cover with foil and bake for 35–45 minutes, uncovering the loaf for the final 10 minutes.

Makes 4–6 servings.

Salmon Loaf with Cheese

Judy, Gorden and Guthrie Schweers   *Ivory Island*

Gorden and Judy either catch their own salmon off the point at Ivory Island or they trade fresh produce with local fishermen who are happy to receive some of the magnificent greens from the Schweerses' unusually prolific garden.

2 cups	cooked salmon, flaked	500 mL
	or	
2	5½ oz (156 mL) tins salmon, undrained	2
1 cup	cottage cheese	250 mL
1 cup	bread crumbs	250 mL
1 tbsp	butter	15 mL
1	small onion, grated	1
1–2 tbsps	minced green pepper	15–25 mL
1	egg, beaten	1
¾ cup	milk	175 mL
¼ tsp	freshly ground pepper	1 mL
⅛ tsp	cayenne	.5 mL
1 tbsp	minced parsley	15 mL
	melted butter, as needed	

Preheat the oven to 350°F (180°C).

Flake the salmon and crush any bones. Stir in the cheese and bread crumbs; mix well. Melt the butter in a skillet and sauté the onion and green pepper until tender. Combine with the salmon mixture. Add the egg, milk, black pepper, cayenne and parsley, stirring thoroughly. Press into a lightly greased or waxed paper-lined 8½" x 4½" (1.5 L) loaf pan. Brush with a little melted butter if desired. Bake for 35–30 minutes uncovered. Let stand for 5 minutes before removing from the pan with a wide spatula. Remove waxed paper. Serve piping hot.

Makes 4–6 servings.

Crispy Coating for Fish

Cynthia, Dennis and Heather Rose   *Ivory Island*

For a light, crispy batter, dip the fish (or chicken or meat) in an egg wash before the coating... and the real secret is to use butter for frying.

1 cup	all-purpose flour	250 mL
1 tbsp	salt	15 mL
¾ tsp	celery salt	4 mL
1½ tsps	garlic powder	7 mL
¾ tsp	freshly ground pepper	4 mL
1½ tsps	dry mustard	7 mL
1 tbsp	paprika	15 mL
¼ tsp	ground ginger	1 mL
¼ tsp	thyme	1 mL
⅛ tsp	basil	.5 mL
⅛ tsp	oregano	.5 mL

Combine all ingredients. Store in a covered container and use as needed.
   Makes enough to coat about 2 lbs (900 g) fish.

Ken's Incredible Barbecue Sauce

Lise, Ken and Noah Brunn   *Langara Point*

¾ cup	corn syrup	175 mL
½ cup	ketchup	125 mL
¼ cup	Worcestershire sauce	50 mL
¼ cup	prepared mustard	50 mL
2 tsps	ground ginger	10 mL
1 tsp	chili powder	5 mL
½–1 tsp	Tabasco sauce (we like it HOT!)	2–5 mL

Shake all the ingredients together and refrigerate until needed.
   Makes about 1¾ cups (425 mL).

Langara Point Smoky Barbecued Salmon

Lise, Ken and Noah Brunn   *Langara Point*

Prepared in Ken's home-built smoker, this salmon could easily be the focal point for almost any celebration. His method is so easy it is hardly a recipe. Just "sprinkle ½ cup (125 mL) brown sugar over each salmon fillet and brush lightly with soy sauce. Marinate for three hours. Pink salmon are excellent this way. Place skin side down on racks and fit into the smoker for approximately one hour. A slower fire might take 1½ hours. Don't turn or otherwise disturb the fillets on the racks while barbecuing because they will flake apart and fall into the fire. They are done when they become a rich red colour. Test with a fork. The pieces will flake apart when done. Don't cook too long in an effort to add more smoke flavour because the salmon flesh will dry out. A slower fire is therefore the best."

Home Smoked Mussels

Lise, Ken and Noah Brunn   *Langara Point*

I really hate smoked mussels! At least the ones my husband carts home from the supermarket around Christmastime. Ugh! They are oily and basically taste like salt and smoke.

So when Lise suggested that we open a container of their own mussels, I must admit I hesitated. But when she produced the small glass jar, the orange-fleshed delicacies were simply glistening inside. The smell of the sea and alder smoke wafted up...my mouth actually began to water.

Not everyone has a ready supply of fresh mussels. I don't. So every time I read this recipe, I become very nostalgic. These mussels have a flavour all their own. This is how you prepare them, in Ken's words.

"This is a 3 day affair, if you also can them.

1. Pick lots of mussels. Place in boiling water for about 10 minutes to steam open. A 5 gallon can on a beach fire seems appropriate and is probably handiest to the mussels anyway. Pick mussels from shells and pack into plastic bags. Discard the shells for the crows. Refrigerate at home until the next day.

2. With a needle and thread, lace mussels about ½" (1 cm) apart and hang in the smoke house. Smoke over alder or any other hardwood for 3–4 hours. Refrigerate until the next day.

3. Pack the mussels tightly into ½ pint (250 mL) jars. Add ¼ tsp (1 mL) salt per jar. Slowly pour olive oil over the mussels until about ¼" (6 mm) deep around the bottom. Process in a pressure canner as you would any other fish (see note). The mussels are best, it seems, when left to age in the jars for about 4 months or until Christmas, whichever comes first."

To Can Fish and Shellfish

Always check the instructions for your pressure canner. The recommended time for processing fish in ½ pint (250 mL) jars is 80 minutes at 15 p.s.i. if altitude is under 3000 feet or 914 metres. The time needed increases with altitude.

Mussels in Mushrooms

Vivian and Bob Bodnar   *Scarlett Point*

All along the British Columbia shoreline are thick clusters of succulent orange-fleshed mussels. Vivian regularly harvests them. There are two types to be found near Scarlett Point, the larger Californian living happily on open, wave-splashed coastlines and its cousin, the common edible mussel *(Mytilus edulis)*, that prefers quieter waters.

Vivian uses a gloved left hand and a screwdriver to pry them off the wave-washed rocks. She says that the smaller ones are more delectable.

This is the Bodnars' favourite mussel dish.

20	whole mussels	20
¼ cup	water	50 mL
20	whole mushrooms	20
¾ cup plus 2 tbsps	butter	200 mL
1 tbsp	vegetable oil	15 mL
5	large garlic cloves, crushed	5
3 tbsps	minced chives or green onion	45 mL
1 tbsp	minced parsley	15 mL
½ tsp	salt	2 mL
¼ tsp	freshly ground pepper	1 mL

Prepare the mussels by scrubbing them thoroughly with a stiff brush. Pull off their "beards" or the bysis with which they cling to the rocks. If you have to hold them for any length of time before cooking, plunge them into a pail of cold water until you are ready to use them. Or refrigerate them in a large plastic bag. Always discard any mussels that do not close when tapped gently—they're dead.

Place the mussels in a large pot that has a lid. Add the water and bring it to a boil. Steam, covered, until the mussels open. Discard any that do not open. Remove with a slotted spoon, removing the meat from each bivalve. Check for any other pieces of beard that may remain on the mussels and gently tear them off. Set aside.

Wash the mushrooms and remove the stems. In a skillet, heat 2 tbsps (25

Scarlett Point

mL) of the butter, the oil and 2 of the garlic cloves. Add the mushroom caps and quickly sauté, uncovered, for about 3 minutes, shaking the pan frequently.

In a small bowl, cream the remaining ¾ cup (175 mL) butter with the remaining garlic, the chives, parsley, salt and pepper. Vivian says that you may also use a food processor for this preparation.

Place 5 mushrooms, cap side downwards, on a scallop shell or small baking dish. Put one or two (if you have lots) mussels on each cap. Top with a generous dollop of garlic butter. Broil for about 1 minute. Serve with fresh crusty bread to sop up all the delicious salty juices.

Makes 4 servings.

Stir-fried Shrimp with Garlic

Judy and Stan Westhaver   *Egg Island*

When I tested this delicious recipe, I served it with freshly made fettuccini, a little of Judy Schweers' Pasta Chuta sauce (p. 53) and lots of freshly grated, pungent Parmesan cheese.

2 tbsps	olive oil	25 mL
1½ lbs	large shrimp, shelled and deveined	680 g
2 tbsps	butter	25 mL
2–3	garlic cloves, minced	2–3
2 tbsps	minced parsley	25 mL
¼ tsp	salt (optional)	1 mL
⅛ tsp	freshly ground pepper	.5 mL
	lemon wedges, as needed	

Heat the oil in a large skillet. Add the shrimp and stir-fry quickly until beginning to turn pink, about 1–2 minutes. Toss in the garlic, parsley, salt and pepper. Continue to cook, stirring constantly, for another 3–4 minutes. Garnish with lemon and serve immediately.

Makes 4–6 servings.

Grilled Scallops

Gwen and Doug Fraser   *Pine Island*

Fire up the barbecue for this one...large succulent scallops with just a hint of garlic and fresh ginger.

2 lbs	large scallops	900 g
	salt and freshly ground pepper,as needed	
½ cup	vegetable oil	125 mL
1	garlic clove, minced	1
3 tbsps	grated fresh ginger	45 mL
¼ cup	soy sauce	50 ml
¼ cup	dry sherry	50 mL
	juice of one lemon	
4	green onions, finely minced	4

Place the scallops in a shallow dish. Sprinkle with salt and pepper. Whisk together the oil, garlic, ginger, soy, sherry, lemon juice and green onions. Pour over the scallops, cover and marinate for one hour. Discard the marinade. Drain the scallops and place them in a barbecue basket or skewer them. Grill about 6″ (15 cm) above the coals for about 5 to 6 minutes per side.

Makes 4–6 servings.

Stir-fried Clams with Vegetables

Cynthia, Dennis and Heather Rose   *Ivory Island*

Dennis' love of music began when he learned to play a harmonica that his father had thrown away. It had four broken reeds, but somehow he managed. Then he graduated to violin and finally the instrument that he played for me at Ivory, a marvellous old five-string banjo, beautifully inlaid and perfectly tuned. We sat in their living room, looking out over the rain-soaked dock where the ship's slickered crew was filling huge oil tanks, and Dennis began to strum tentatively. Very shortly the music began to flow and a rousing "breakdown" echoed through the small house.

Cynthia uses small butter clams for this recipe. She says that the larger the clam, the tougher it is.

2 tbsps	vegetable oil	25 mL
2 tbsps	minced garlic	25 mL
1	medium onion, chopped	1
½	green pepper, diced	½
1 cup	clams, steamed from the shell, or canned clams	250 mL
4–6 cups	diagonally sliced carrots, celery and bok choy	1–1.5 L
2 tbsps	oyster sauce	25 mL
1 tbsp	cornstarch	15 mL
½ cup	water or stock	125 mL

Heat the vegetable oil in a wok or heavy skillet until very hot. Stir in the garlic, onion and pepper. Cook, stirring constantly, for 1 minute. Add the clams and stir-fry for another minute. Toss in the vegetables and continue to stir-fry until barely tender crisp, about 2–4 minutes.

Combine the oyster sauce, cornstarch and water. Pour into the wok, stirring until thickened slightly and glazed. Serve on a bed of steamed rice.

Makes 2–4 servings.

To enjoy sea urchin roe, open the urchin over the sink, protecting your hands from the sharp spines with rubber gloves. Remove the five soft orange gonads and rinse them with a little pear cider if you have some. Simply put them on a plate and squeeze some fresh lemon over them. Judy feels "it's a crime to add a lot of spices." Instead she simply "smooths them on crackers" to enjoy "the beautiful essence of the food, just the way it was made." (Judy Schweers, Ivory Island)

Vegetarian Shepherd's Pie

Kathy Heise and Lance Barrett-Lennard   *Boat Bluff*

Kathy and Lance's study of whales has led them to string a microphone into the water at a depth of about 100 feet. The small speaker sits on top of their refrigerator so that when a pod of whales pass by their songs echo throughout the kitchen. Meanwhile, Kathy fills her hand with peanuts, sticks it out the window and feeds a pair of Steller's jays.

Filled with a rich gravy-like sauce, this dish is simply loaded with nutritious ingredients.

1 cup	dry green lentils	250 mL
3 cups	stock, tomato juice or water	750 mL
¼ cup	sesame seeds	50 mL
1 tbsp	Worcestershire sauce	15 mL
2 tsps	soy sauce, preferably tamari	10 mL
¼ cup	butter	50 mL
2	medium onions, chopped	2
¼ tsp	rubbed savory	1 mL
¼ tsp	tarragon	1 mL
⅛ tsp	freshly grated nutmeg	.5 mL
¼ cup	wholewheat flour	50 mL
1 cup	milk	250 mL
2 cups	cooked leftover vegetables such as carrots, peas or green beans	500 mL
5 cups	mashed potatoes (see below) melted butter, as needed	1.25 L

Simmer the lentils and stock together in a heavy saucepan until the lentils are tender, about 45 minutes.

While the lentils simmer, boil 6 medium potatoes in lightly salted water until tender. Drain and whip with ½ cup (125 mL) milk, ⅓ cup (75 mL) butter, ½ tsp (2 mL) salt and 3 tbsps (45 mL) wheat germ. Set aside.

Stir the sesame seeds, Worcestershire and soy sauce into the cooked lentils. Set aside.

Melt the butter in a skillet and sauté the onions until they begin to wilt. Season with the savory, tarragon and nutmeg. Stir in the flour and continue to cook until the flour mixture bubbles. Whisk in the milk, cooking until thickened. Stir into the lentils with the cooked vegetables.

Preheat the oven to 350°F (180°C).

Butter a 3 quart (3 L) casserole and pat in about half the mashed potatoes to form a 1" (2.5 cm) thick crust. Pour in the filling and cover with the remaining potatoes, hiding the lentils from view. Brush with a little melted butter. Bake for 35–45 minutes or until the crust is golden on the surface.

Makes 6–8 hearty servings.

Quadra Island Pizza Dough

Wendy, Jim, Jessie and Melissa Abram   *Cape Mudge*

Scrumptious!!!!!! Wendy suggests that a quick pizza sauce may be made by thinning out tomato paste with water and adding chopped onion, oregano, garlic, basil, salt and pepper. She then simmers it for a few minutes before spreading it over her pizza crusts.

1 tbsp	active dry yeast	15 mL
½ cup	lukewarm water	125 mL
2 tsps	granulated sugar	10 mL
½ cup	milk	125 mL
¼ cup	softened shortening	50 mL
1½ tsps	salt	7 mL
2½–3 cups	all-purpose flour	625–750 mL

Combine the yeast, water and 1 tsp (5 mL) of the sugar in a large mixing bowl. Let stand for 7–10 minutes. Stir in the milk, shortening, salt and remaining sugar. Beat in the flour, a cupful at a time, reserving a bit for kneading the dough. When the flour has been incorporated, turn the dough out onto a floured surface and knead for 5–10 minutes or until very smooth and elastic. Grease a mixing bowl and turn the dough in it to coat all sides. Cover and allow it to rise until doubled, about 45 minutes. Punch down and cut into 2 pieces. Roll each piece until it fits your pizza pan.

At this point the crust may be wrapped tightly and frozen or spread with toppings and baked at 400°F (200°C) for 20 minutes.

Makes two 12" (30 cm) pizza crusts.

Cornbread Tamale Pie

Linda and Don Weeden   *Cape Scott*

This is one of those recipes that quickly becomes a family standby.

1 lb	ground beef	450 g
1	onion, diced	1
1 10 oz tin	tomato soup	1 284 mL tin
1 cup	water	250 mL
¼ tsp	freshly ground pepper	1 mL
1 tsp	salt	5 mL
1 tbsp	chili powder	15 mL
1 cup	corn kernels (canned, fresh or frozen)	250 mL
½ cup	chopped green pepper	125 mL

Topping

¾ cup	yellow corn meal	175 mL
1 tbsp	all-purpose flour	15 mL
1 tbsp	granulated sugar	15 mL
1½ tsps	baking powder	7 mL
1	egg, beaten	1
⅓ cup	milk	75 mL
1 tbsp	vegetable oil	15 mL

Preheat the oven to 425°F (220°C).

In a heavy skillet, sauté the beef until brown. Stir in the onion and continue to cook until the onion is transparent. Add the tomato soup, water, pepper, salt, chili powder, corn and green pepper. Bring to a boil and simmer for 15 minutes while you prepare the topping.

In a large mixing bowl, stir together the corn meal, flour, sugar and baking powder. Whisk the egg, milk and oil together. Add to the dry ingredients.

Lightly grease a 2 quart (2 L) casserole. Pour in the meat filling and top with the cornbread mixture. Bake for 20–25 minutes or until the cornbread is beginning to brown.

Makes 6–8 servings.

Parmesan Cheese Pasta Sauce with Miso

Judy, Gorden and Guthrie Schweers   *Ivory Island*

If you have never used miso, this is the best recipe with which to begin. Barley miso is very mild and well suited to our North American taste buds. It is made with cooked barley and soybeans, which are fermented using a yogurt-like culture to create a wonderful sweet/sour/salty taste. Very high in protein, miso contains all 17 essential amino acids, thus aiding digestion. But best of all, it tastes great. Even my picky sons loved this sauce, which I served over homemade noodles.

2 tbsps	butter	25 mL
2	garlic cloves, minced	2
1 tbsp	minced fresh parsley	15 mL
2 tbsps	all-purpose flour	25 ml
1½ cups	milk	375 mL
1 tbsp	barley miso	15 mL
½ cup	Parmesan cheese	125 mL
1 tsp	ground anise or whole anise seed	5 mL

| ½ tsp | cayenne pepper (optional) | 2 mL |
| | cooked egg noodles | |

In a non-stick skillet, melt the butter. Stir in the garlic and the parsley; sauté for 1–2 minutes. Sprinkle on the flour and continue to cook, stirring, for about 30 seconds or until the mixture begins to bubble. Whisk in the milk and the miso, cooking over medium-low heat until smooth. Stir in the cheese, anise and cayenne pepper. Serve over hot egg noodles.

Makes 4 servings.

Pasta Chuta

Judy, Gorden and Guthrie Schweers   *Ivory Island*

Judy hails from California, where she earned her Home Economics degree. This is her mom's innovative version of spaghetti sauce which Judy cooks quite often. In the grey northern winters I can imagine that it would be a welcome dish.

1 lb	lean ground beef	450 g
4	large carrots, peeled	4
½ cup	minced fresh parsley	125 mL
2	medium onions, peeled	2
3	garlic cloves, peeled	3
2 tbsps	olive oil	25 mL
7 cups	tomato sauce	1.75 L
	or	
2 28 oz tins	tomato sauce	2 796 mL tins
2 oz	dried black mushrooms (see below)	50 g
½ tsp	cinnamon	2 mL
½ tsp	ground ginger	2 mL
½ tsp	allspice	2 mL
3	bay leaves	3
½ tsp	ground cloves	2 mL
	cooked pasta	

Dried black mushrooms come in various types of packages—some without weights imprinted. You will need about 2 cups (500 mL) for this recipe. They are found in Oriental food markets.

Sauté the ground beef in a skillet until browned. Set aside. Grind the carrots, parsley, onions and garlic together or chop them all very finely. Heat the oil in a large saucepan or Dutch oven. Add the vegetables and cook, stirring, until they begin to brown. Transfer the meat to the vegetable mixture, scraping off any brown bits from the skillet. Stir in the tomato sauce, mushrooms and spices. Bring to a boil, reduce the heat and simmer for 2–3 hours or until thickened. Taste and correct the seasoning. Serve over steaming pasta, passing grated cheese to be sprinkled over each serving, if desired.

Makes 5–6 cups (1.25–1.5 L).

Spanokopita

Janet, Jerry, Jake and Justine Etzkorn   *Carmanah Point*

Janet's little plastic greenhouse provides fresh kale, spinach and chard almost all year round. Long raised beds are full of wonderful vegetables in the summertime and the perimeter of the property is thick with salmonberries, blackberries and salal.

Spanokopita is a Greek dish which may be served either crispy and fragrant from the oven or chilled as an interesting addition to a salad plate. It is made with phyllo pastry which is tissue-thin dough, sold fresh or frozen at many European or Mediterranean grocery stores. Feta cheese, another ingredient, is sometimes quite salty. Taste it and rinse it under cold water if necessary to tone down the flavour a little. You may not need to add any salt at all to this recipe.

2 tbsps	butter	25 mL
1	small cooking onion, chopped	1
¼ cup	minced green onions	50 mL
6–8 quarts	fresh spinach, chard and/or kale, chopped	6–8 L
	or	
2 10 oz pkgs	frozen spinach, thawed, drained well and chopped	2 300 g pkgs
2 tbsps	minced fresh parsley	25 mL
1 tbsp	dried or fresh dillweed	15 mL
1 tsp	salt (optional)	5 mL
¼ tsp	freshly ground pepper	1 mL
¼ cup	milk	50 mL
3	eggs	3
½ lb	feta cheese	225 g
½ cup	unsalted butter	125 mL
½ lb	phyllo pastry, thawed	225 g

Preheat the oven to 350°F (180°C).

Melt the 2 tbsps (25 mL) butter in a large saucepan over medium heat.

Sauté the onion until golden. Toss in the green onions and continue to cook until they are wilted. Stir in the spinach, chard and/or kale. Season with parsley, dill, salt and pepper, tossing lightly. Cover and cook until the greens are tender, about 4–6 minutes. Drain off any excess liquid (it should be moist but not swimming in juices) and chop the vegetables finely. Stir in the milk.

Beat the eggs lightly and combine with the cheese. Stir into the spinach mixture and set aside.

Melt the ½ cup (125 mL) unsalted butter. With a wide pastry brush, paint butter on the bottom and sides of a 8″ x 12″ (3 L) baking dish. Lay one sheet of phyllo across the width of the pan, brush with melted butter, and repeat until you have used 8 sheets of pastry. Pour in the spinach mixture and spread evenly. Layer another 8 sheets of pastry over the filling, buttering each generously. Refrigerate the unused phyllo pastry in tightly sealed plastic. With a very sharp knife, divide the spanokopita into serving sections by cutting through the top 5 or 6 layers.

Bake, uncovered, for 45 minutes or until deep golden brown. Let stand for 10 minutes to set a little before serving.

Makes 8–10 generous servings.

Mung Dal

Judy, Gorden and Guthrie Schweers　　　　　　　　　　　　　　　*Ivory Island*

Garlicky and delicious, this spread is perfect served with Middle Eastern flat bread such as pita, or with ultra-thin slices of Miso Bread (p. 75).

1 cup	mung beans	250 mL
4 cups	vegetable or chicken stock	1 L
3 tbsps	vegetable oil	45 mL
2	garlic cloves, minced	2
1	medium onion, diced	1
1 1″ piece	fresh ginger, peeled and grated	1 2.5 cm piece
1 tsp	turmeric	5 mL
1–2 tsps	curry powder	5–10 mL

Simmer the beans in the stock until tender, about 35–40 minutes. Set aside. Heat the oil in a skillet and gently sauté the garlic, onion and ginger for 5 minutes. Stir in the spices and add the mixture to the beans. Cook over medium heat for an additional 10 minutes, stirring occasionally. Serve hot with rice or at room temperature as a spread. Garnish with minced green onion and snipped flat parsley.

Makes about 5 cups (1.25 L).

Dumplings for Stew

Dan and Fil McMurray   *Pointer Island (now automated)*

From their deck on Pointer Island, the McMurrays could watch whales spout. They loved their tiny island, and grew everything from exotic Chinese vegetables to turnips and potatoes. They tried to be as self-sufficient as possible. The day I visited, Dan was constantly excusing himself to check on the salmon he was canning.

There is a happy ending to their automation story: they accepted a posting at Green Island, just north of Prince Rupert, within sight of Alaska. At last report, Dan had cultivated a huge garden and was raising chickens.

1½ cups	all-purpose flour	375 mL
3 tsps	baking powder	15 mL
½ tsp	sage	2 mL
1 tsp	dried parsley	5 mL
¼ tsp	salt	1 mL
2 tsps	butter	10 mL
¾ cup	cold water	175 mL

In a medium-sized mixing bowl, stir together the flour, baking powder, sage, parsley and salt. Cut in the butter. Stir in the cold water, adding more if necessary to make a thick batter. Drop by tablespoons into briskly boiling stew. Cover, and continue to cook for 5 minutes. Remove the lid and cook for 2 or 3 minutes longer. Serve immediately.

Makes about 8 dumplings.

Stuffed Flank Steak with Red Wine Sauce

Gwen and Doug Fraser   *Pine Island*

This is one of the Frasers' favourite wintertime meals, hearty and particularly good with freshly steamed carrots and tender-crisp green beans.

1	2½ lb (1.35 kg) flank steak	1

Stuffing

2½ cups	bread cubes (about 5 slices)	625 mL
¼ cup	vegetable oil	50 mL
2 tbsps	butter	25 mL
1 lb	ground beef	450 g
2	eggs	2
¾ cup	minced onion	175 mL
2 tbsps	minced parsley	25 mL

1	garlic clove, minced	1
1 tsp	salt	5 mL
½ tsp	freshly ground pepper	2 mL
¼ tsp	dried thyme, crumbled	1 mL

Red Wine Sauce

1 tbsp	vegetable oil	15 mL
1 tbsp	butter	15 mL
¾ cup	finely diced carrots	175 mL
¾ cup	minced onion	175 mL
1	tomato, coarsely chopped	1
2	bay leaves	2
1 tsp	dried thyme	5 mL
1 cup	beef stock or water	250 mL
1 cup	dry red wine	250 mL
2 tbsps	arrowroot flour	25 mL
¼ cup	water	50 mL
	salt and freshly ground pepper, to taste	

Cut the steak lengthwise with a sharp paring knife to make a pocket for the stuffing. Gwen suggests keeping the steak flat on a cutting board with one hand so that you can better "feel" the knife sliding through the meat. Lift the upper "lip" and cut again, keeping your blade horizontal and being careful not to cut through either end. Set aside while preparing the stuffing.

Brown the bread in ¼ cup (50 mL) of the oil and 2 tbsps (25 mL) of the butter in a large skillet. Turn into a bowl and add the ground beef, eggs, onion, parsley, garlic, salt, pepper and thyme. Mix lightly to combine. Stuff the steak tightly, filling it to the corners. Bring the lower "lip" up over the filling, then pull the upper "lip" down to cover the stuffing. Shape into a loaf, tying securely with string.

Heat the remaining oil and butter in the skillet and brown the rolled steak evenly. Toss in the carrots, minced onion, tomato, bay leaves and thyme. Cook gently, uncovered, for 5 minutes. Pour in the stock and red wine. Bring to a boil, cover, and reduce the heat.

Place meat and sauce in a covered pan and braise gently for 1½ hours, turning occasionally. Lift the meat onto a heated serving platter. Keep warm while finishing the sauce.

Skim any fat from the cooking liquid. Mix the arrowroot with the water and pour into the simmering sauce. Cook and stir until thickened. Season to taste with salt and pepper. Pour over and around the meat. Slice and serve.

Makes 8–10 servings.

Cipaille

Lina, Jean, Isabelle and François Beaudet   *Bonilla Island*

Although I have not tested this interesting heritage recipe, I have included it because it harks back to the Beaudets' roots in the Laurentian Shield. It is one of the classics in French Canadian cooking. A huge meat pie, large enough to feed the hungriest family, it is made with the game that flourished in the mountains of Québec and it is baked slowly (traditionally in a wood-fired oven).

Filling

1	hare, skinned and cleaned	1
2	partridges	2
	or	
3 lbs	chicken pieces	1.3 kg
2 lbs	moose or beef, cut into cubes	900 g
2 lbs	pork, cut into cubes	900 g
½ bottle	dry red wine	½ bottle
6	large onions, chopped	6
2 tsps	salt	10 mL
1	bay leaf	1
½ tsp each	ground cloves, cinnamon, black pepper, savory, thyme, chervil	2 mL each
6–8	medium potatoes, peeled and sliced	6–8

Flaky Pastry

8 cups	all-purpose flour	2 L
2 tsps	salt	10 mL
¾ cup	grated sharp cheese	175 mL
3⅓ cup	lard or shortening	825 mL
1 cup	ice water	250 mL

In a large non-metallic bowl, combine the meat, wine, onions and seasonings. Cover with plastic wrap and refrigerate for 12–24 hours.

Measure the flour, salt and cheese into a large mixing bowl. Cut in the lard or shortening until the mixture is crumbly. With a fork, stir in the ice water until the dough holds its shape. Gather into a ball and refrigerate until you are ready to use it.

Roll the dough to ¼" (6 mm) thickness on a floured surface. Cover the bottom and sides of a large roasting pan with a layer of dough. Put in a layer of rabbit and then a layer of potatoes. Top with another layer of pastry. Add the partridge, more potatoes and another layer of dough. Alternate the remaining meat with potatoes and pastry, ending with a pastry topping.

Bake in a *preheated* 250°F (120°C) oven for 10–12 hours.

Orange Glazed Spareribs

Judy and Stan Westhaver   *Egg Island*

Over the years many have heard Judy or Stan on the radio advising fishermen on the wisdom of sailing on that particular day. Last Christmas, Judy received a bottle of Grand Marnier from one of those grateful listeners, a sailor to whom she had never spoken, but who nevertheless appreciated the information she so willingly gave to all who asked. It's hard to say whether any lives have been saved—one can never count "what-ifs"—but undoubtedly many wives and mothers of fishermen have spent fewer hours worrying by the kitchen window.

4 lbs	pork side ribs	1.8 kg
	lightly salted water, as needed	
1	6½ oz (175 mL) tin orange juice	1
	concentrate, thawed	
1–2	garlic cloves, crushed	1–2
2 tsps	Worcestershire sauce	10 mL
½ tsp	salt	2 mL
¼ tsp	freshly ground pepper	1 mL
1	orange, sliced into rounds	1
	fresh parsley	

Cover the spareribs with salted water in a large kettle or Dutch oven. Bring to a boil, cover and reduce the heat. Simmer until the meat is almost tender, about 1 hour. Drain well.

Preheat the oven to 350°F (180°C).

In a small bowl, whisk together the orange juice concentrate, garlic, Worcestershire, salt and pepper. Place the spareribs in a shallow baking pan and pour half the sauce over them. Roast uncovered for 30–40 minutes, basting frequently with the remaining sauce. The ribs will be glazed, brown and quite delicately flavoured. Garnish with fresh orange slices and parsley.

Makes 6–8 generous servings.

Baked Stuffed Venison Heart

Karen and John Coldwell   *McInnes Island*

For me a venison heart was impossible to obtain, so I am offering Karen's recipe verbatim, without testing. Many of the keepers shoot their own venison, while others like the Schweerses just explain loudly to the deer that invade their garden that if they don't "shoo," they'll be eaten. Everyone has a way of coping with the overabundance of animals on the lights.

1	venison heart, soaked overnight in salted water	1
	toasted bread crumbs	
1	small onion, minced	1
	poultry seasoning, as needed	
	boiling water, as needed	
	bacon strips, as needed	
¼ cup	water	50 ml

Karen writes: "I toast the bread the way my father did, in a slow oven (150–200°F/70–100°C), turning once, until the bread is lightly browned and dry. Wholewheat bread is the best and I usually use 4 slices. Finely grind the toasted bread in the blender. Add the onion and the seasonings you would use for poultry—marjoram, thyme, pepper and salt, but not too much sage. Gradually add *boiling* water until the dressing is moist but not soggy. Stuff into the heart and place in a covered casserole. Lay about 4 bacon strips on top of the heart, add ¼ cup (50 mL) water, cover and bake at 325°F (150°C) for approximately 3 hours or until the heart is tender. Baking time depends on the size of the heart but it must be baked slowly. Any extra dressing can be placed around the outside of the heart during the cooking."

Karen doesn't specify just how many people this dish will serve, but I would guess 3–4.

The Staff of Life:
Yeast Breads, Rolls and
Sweet Breads

Pointer Island

Sisters Island White Bread

Dan Earl   *Sisters Island*

Sisters Island is a small piece of barren rock, without even a touch of green. Once a mountain top, it has lost none of its primeval feeling. Seals, starfish, birds and lightkeepers are its only inhabitants. Often battered by gales, it is one of the rotational stations that has keepers who stay for only two weeks at a time. No one could really manage longer.

Dan Earl bakes all their bread using British Columbia's wonderfully delicate fireweed honey. Fireweed is the plant that grows in profusion after a clearcut or a forest fire, so BC has lots of it. But you can use any light-flavoured wildflower honey in this recipe.

6 cups	warm water	1.5 L
4	eggs, beaten	4
3 tbsps	fast-rising yeast	45 mL
2 tbsps	salt	25 mL
¾ cup	fireweed honey	175 mL
12–14 cups	unbleached all-purpose white flour	3–3.5 L

In a very large mixing bowl, combine the warm water, eggs, yeast, salt and honey. Mix thoroughly with a wooden spoon. Let stand for 10 minutes. Add the flour, a cupful (250 mL) at a time, beating well after each addition until it leaves the sides of the bowl. Turn the dough out onto a well-floured board. Knead it thoroughly for 5–7 minutes or until it is smooth and elastic. Wash the mixing bowl and grease it and the dough generously. Return the dough to the bowl, cover and allow the dough to rise *at room temperature* until it has doubled in bulk. Punch it down well and allow it to rise again.

Divide the dough into six portions and shape into loaves. Place in well-greased pans and cut diagonally to the bottom of each loaf several times. Let rise again at room temperature until doubled. Bake in a preheated 350°F (180°C) oven about 30 minutes or until golden. Watch carefully as the honey in this bread can cause it to brown very quickly in the final minutes of baking.

Makes 6 loaves.

Anadama Bread

Gwen and Doug Fraser   *Pine Island*

This recipe is from one of the best bakers of all the lightstations, Gwen Fraser. She and her husband Doug are in charge of Pine Island's new light—the old one was washed away by a gale thirteen years ago. Located at the southern end of Queen Charlotte Sound, it is a familiar and comforting sight to those who have cruised the inside passage to Alaska.

5 cups	all-purpose flour	1.25 L
2½ tsps	salt	12 mL
1 cup	yellow corn meal	250 mL
2 tbsps	active dry yeast	25 mL
¼ cup	softened margarine	50 mL
2 cups	very hot water	500 mL
½ cup	molasses	125 mL

In a very large bowl combine 2½ cups (625 mL) of the flour, the salt, corn meal and yeast. Gradually add the softened margarine, the hot water and the molasses. Beat for 2 minutes at medium speed. Add ½ cup (125 mL) more of the flour and beat at high speed for 2 minutes. The batter should be very thick. Stir in enough of the remaining flour to make a soft dough. Turn out onto a floured surface and knead for 8–10 minutes. Rotate in a greased bowl to moisten the dough. Cover and let rise in a warm place until doubled in bulk, about 1 hour. Punch down, shape into two loaves and place in well-greased 9" x 5" (2 L) loaf pans. Let rise again for 45 minutes. Bake in a preheated 375°F (190°C) oven for 35 minutes or until golden brown.

Makes 2 loaves.

Yeast Cornbread

Dan and Fil McMurray   *Pointer Island (now automated)*

Dan and Fil (short for Filamena) grind all their own flour in a mill that Dan has enclosed with yew wood. They buy their grain from Winnipeg and store it until they need it. While I visited, we ground a batch. There is something "little red hen-ish" and indeed, very satisfying, about scooping handfuls of wheat from a bucket, grinding it into flour and then baking golden loaves of bread.

1 cup	milk	250 mL
6 tbsps	granulated sugar	90 mL
2 tsps	salt	10 mL
½ cup	butter or margarine	125 mL
½ cup	very warm water	125 mL
2 tbsps	active dry yeast	25 mL
2	eggs, beaten	2
3½ cups	all-purpose flour	875 mL
1¾ cups	yellow corn meal	425 mL

Scald the milk in a heavy-bottomed saucepan. Stir in the sugar, salt and butter. Let cool to lukewarm.

Measure the warm water into a large mixing bowl. Sprinkle with the yeast, stirring until dissolved. Pour in the lukewarm milk mixture, beaten eggs, flour and corn meal. Beat by hand or with a heavy-duty mixer for about 2 minutes. The batter will be quite stiff. Turn into two well-greased 8½" x 4½" (1.5 L) loaf pans. Cover and let rise until double, about 1–1½ hours.

Bake in a preheated 375°F (190°C) oven until golden brown.

Makes two loaves.

Gwen's Crunchy Cracked Wheat Bread

Gwen and Doug Fraser   *Pine Island*

Doug simply raves about this bread...it is his all-time favourite.

¼ cup	granulated sugar	50 mL
½ cup	warm water	125 mL
2 tbsps	active dry yeast	25 mL
1 tbsp	salt	15 mL
¼ cup	melted shortening	50 mL
2 tbsps	molasses	25 mL
4 cups	hot water	1 L
2½ cups	cracked wheat	625 mL
9–10 cups	all-purpose flour	2.25–2.5L

Stir 1 tsp (5 mL) of the sugar and the warm water together in a small bowl. Sprinkle with the yeast. Let stand for 10 minutes, until puffed. Stir well.

Dissolve the remaining sugar, salt, shortening and molasses in the hot water. Add the cracked wheat and cool to lukewarm. Stir in the yeast mixture. Add half the flour, beating well. Mix in the remaining flour. You may have to work in the last of the flour with your hands. Turn the dough onto a floured surface and knead for 8–10 minutes or until smooth and elastic. Shape into two balls and place into well-greased bowls, turning to grease the surface of the dough. Cover and let rise in a warm place until doubled in bulk, about 1 hour.

Punch down and let rise again for 30 minutes. Divide into 4 equal portions and shape into loaves. Place in greased 9" x 5" (2 L) loaf pans.

Cover and let rise in a warm place until doubled, about another hour. Bake in a *preheated* 400°F (200°C) oven for 30 minutes or until golden brown and hollow sounding when tapped.

Makes 4 loaves.

Pine Island Graham Granola Bread

Gwen and Doug Fraser   *Pine Island*

This is another winner from Gwen Fraser...and about the best bread my family has ever tasted!!!

Gwen suggests grinding the granola in a food processor or blender before measuring.

1½ tbsps	active dry yeast	20 mL
1 tbsp	granulated sugar	15 mL
1½ cups	warm water	375 mL
1 cup	buttermilk	250 mL
¼ cup	unsalted butter	50 mL
¼ cup	liquid honey	50 mL
1¼ cups	graham flour	300 mL
1 cup	ground granola cereal	250 mL
½ cup	rolled oats	125 mL
½ cup	finely chopped walnuts or sunflower seeds	125 mL
1½ tsps	salt	7 mL
1	egg, beaten	1
3½–4 cups	all-purpose flour	875 mL–1 L

In a small bowl, stir together the yeast, sugar and ½ cup (125 mL) of the warm water. Let stand for 10 minutes or until puffed.

Heat the remaining water in a heavy saucepan. Add the buttermilk, butter and honey, stirring until the butter is melted. Remove from the heat and cool to lukewarm.

In a large bowl combine the graham flour, granola, oats, walnuts and salt. Add the yeast puff, the beaten egg and the other liquid ingredients. Whisk until the batter is thick and smooth, about 5 minutes.

Using a wooden spoon, beat in the all-purpose flour a cupful at a time until a soft dough is formed. Scrape out onto a well-floured board and knead until smooth and elastic. Knead in additional flour if necessary.

Wash and grease the bread bowl. Add the dough, turning to coat the entire surface. Let rise in a warm place until doubled in bulk, about 1 hour. Punch down and let rise again. The second rising will only take about 45 minutes. Cut the dough in half and shape into two loaves. Place in well-greased 9″ x 5″ (2 L) loaf pans, cover lightly and allow to rise again until doubled. Bake in a preheated 375°F (190°C) oven for 40 minutes or until golden.

Makes 2 loaves.

Sunflower Bran Bread

Gwen and Doug Fraser   *Pine Island*

Gwen and Doug buy everything by the case and when the choice is available, they purchase organic ingredients from suppliers like the Seed of Life and the Pacific Share Cooperative. They have made a conscious decision to produce healthy food.

2 tbsps	active dry yeast	25 mL
½ cup	warm water	125 mL
2 tbsps	granulated sugar	25 mL
⅓ cup	molasses	75 ml
¼ cup	unsalted butter, at room temperature	50 mL
1½ cups	milk	375 mL
5–5½ cups	unbleached all-purpose flour	1250–1375 mL
1½ cups	natural bran	375 mL
½ cup	sunflower seeds	125 mL
1 tbsp	salt	15 mL

Combine the yeast, warm water and sugar in a small bowl. Let stand until puffed, about 10 minutes. Heat the molasses, butter and milk together over low heat, until the butter is almost melted and the liquid is lukewarm.

In a large bowl, stir together 2 cups (500 mL) of the flour, the bran, sunflower seeds and salt. Whisk in the yeast and milk mixtures, beating until smooth, about 3 minutes. Using a wooden spoon, mix in the remaining flour, a half cupful (125 mL) at a time, until a soft dough is formed. Knead for 5–7 minutes on a heavily floured surface until smooth and elastic, adding flour as needed. Wash and grease the mixing bowl. Place the dough into it, turning to coat it with shortening. Cover and let rise until doubled in a warm, draft free place, about 1½–2 hours. Punch down and turn out onto a floured surface. Let rest for 10 minutes. Cut into two pieces, shape into loaves and place, seam side down, in 9" x 5" (2 L) loaf pans. Cover and let rise until doubled again, about 1–1¼ hours. Bake in a *preheated* 375°F (190°C) oven for 45 minutes or until well browned. Remove from the pans immediately.

Makes 2 loaves.

Queen Charlotte Wholewheat Bread

Lise, Ken and Noah Brunn   *Langara Island*

Langara is perched on a rocky cliff at the northern tip of the Queen Charlotte Islands. It seems like a place lost in time. The storms are so wild and fierce, with winds up to 80–160 k.p.h not uncommon, that the engine room, a full 100 feet above the water was severely damaged by a storm-whipped sea.

The Charlottes have been compared with the Galapagos in that they are the only place on earth where certain plants and fishes are found. It also appears that during the ice age the islands might have been the final North American refuge for certain mosses found in lands as far away as Great Britain, western Ireland and Borneo.

The day I was there was the same one that a huge work crew arrived to fix various things around the station. We drank mugs of Lise's wonderful coffee and we ate thick slices of this homemade bread, lightly buttered and topped with her own home-smoked mussels...it was a meal to remember.

¾ cup	softened butter	175 mL
3¾ cups	very hot water	875 mL
2	eggs	2
1 cup	skim milk powder	250 mL
1 tbsp	salt	15 mL
¼ cup	warm water	50 mL
1 tsp	granulated sugar	5 mL
2 tbsps	active dry yeast	25 mL
9½–10 cups	wholewheat flour	2375–2500 mL
½ cup	Sunny Boy or Red River cereal	125 mL
1 tbsp	caraway (optional)	15 mL

Lise instructed me to make sure that the house was warm before beginning to make the bread.

In a large bowl, stir together the butter and hot water. When the butter is melted, whisk in the eggs, salt and skim milk powder.

Measure the warm water into a small bowl. Stir in the white sugar and sprinkle on the yeast. Allow it to puff for 10 minutes.

Whisk the yeast mixture into the first bowl. Add 4 cups (1 L) of the flour to make a sloppy batter, beating with an electric mixer for 5 minutes. Beat in the cereal, caraway and more flour, a bit at a time, until the dough is very thick. Turn out onto a floured board and knead for 10 minutes.

Wash and grease the large bowl. Return the bread to it, greasing the top generously. Cover and allow to rise for 2 hours or until doubled. Punch down and let it rise a second time for approximately 1½ hours. Cut the dough into loaves and place in well-greased bread pans. Let rise again before baking in a preheated 350°F (180°C) oven for about 1 hour. Lise shapes her bread into rounds and bakes several loaves in her favourite cast iron skillets.

Makes two large 10" (25 cm) loaves baked in cast iron skillets *or* two 9" x 5" (2 L) loaves plus one round loaf.

Very Light 100% Wholewheat Bread

Pauline, Joe and Cindy Balmer   *Estevan Point*

Lightkeepers are often a forgotten lot. The saying "out of sight, out of mind" is quite appropriate. And on a less accessible station such as Estevan Point, it really rings true. Pauline has never been able to vote in a provincial election: to her knowledge they are not even registered. Rarely do the people in the rest of the country glimpse, much less understand, the people of the lights.

Most people think that keepers work their eight-hour shifts and then drive home. This is indeed the case at many lightstations in the eastern part of the nation. But on the Pacific coast, it is the exception rather than the rule. I'd like to see anyone try to drive to "civilization" from Estevan Point or Ivory Island or Sisters. It is troubling to the lightkeepers who work long, long hours to be taken so much for granted, and then to be told that their services could be replaced by automation. It is the ultimate insult to be told they are expendable by bureaucrats who have never, not even once, visited their station.

Pauline says that she doesn't know why this bread is so light, but she thinks it may be the lecithin, which may be purchased from most health food stores.

5 cups	warm water	1.25 L
2 tbsps	liquid honey	25 mL
3 tbsps	active dry yeast	45 mL
11–13 cups	wholewheat flour	2.75–3.25L
¼ cup	vegetable oil	50 mL
4 tsps	salt	20 mL
¼ cup	molasses	50 mL
2 tbsps	soy lecithin	25 mL

Pour the water into a very large mixing bowl. Stir in the honey and sprinkle in the yeast so that it dissolves. Let stand for 5–10 minutes to allow the yeast to puff. Beat in 4 cups (1 L) of the flour. Add the oil, salt, molasses and lecithin, combining thoroughly. Gradually knead in the remaining flour, just until the dough stops sticking to your hands. Gather up into a ball and place in a well-greased bowl. Oil the top of the dough and cover with a kitchen towel. Let rise in a warm place until doubled. Punch down and allow it to rise again. When doubled, punch down and cut into 4 pieces. Shape into loaves and place into greased 8½" x 4½" (1.5 L) loaf pans. Cover and let rise until doubled. Bake in a preheated 375°F (190°C) oven for 30 minutes or until golden brown.

Makes 4 loaves.

Sourdough Starter

Used for many years by early settlers and prospectors, this type of bread starter was often passed from one household to another. It is the most basic form of yeast but nowadays, we use it mainly to enrich a baked product rather than depending on it for leavening.

1 tbsp	active dry yeast	15 mL
2 cups	warm water	500 mL
3 tbsps	granulated sugar	45 mL
1 tsp	salt	5 mL
2 cups	all-purpose flour	500 mL

Dissolve the yeast in the warm water. Stir in the sugar and the salt. Beat in the flour by hand. Pour the batter into an empty shortening tin or a similar size container with a lid. Leave the batter, covered, at room temperature for 3 days, stirring it down each day. By this time it should have a sour smell. Refrigerate it.

Every day or so, "feed it" the following ingredients, leaving it for a few hours before using it in any recipe.

1 cup	milk	250 mL
1 cup	all-purpose flour	250 mL
½ cup	granulated sugar	125 mL

Note: If you need to go away, the starter can be left without feeding for about 4 or 5 days. To leave for a longer period, freeze the entire container. On returning, thaw it at room temperature, feed it, and then put it back into the refrigerator.

Sisters Island

Sourdough Wholewheat Bread

Barbara Spence   *Entrance Island*

The thin coating of soil on Entrance Island was transported by barge from
nearby Gabriola Island. It supports only low growing shrubs, a few
wildflowers and grass. Growing a garden is very, very difficult because of the
lack of fresh water and the blazing sun which beats down from morning till
dusk on the treeless landscape.

The age of a settler's sourdough was once a matter of pride among the
old-timers, who often hung it from the rafters to store it. It was used so
widely during the gold rush days that the name "sourdough" was applied to
any adventurer who tried to find his overnight fortune in the Klondike.

1 cup	lukewarm water	250 mL
1 tsp	granulated sugar	5 mL
1 tbsp	active dry yeast	15 mL
2 cups	sourdough starter (p. 69)	500 mL
2	eggs, lightly beaten	2
¼ cup	molasses	50 mL
1 tbsp	liquid honey	15 mL
1 tbsp	salt	15 mL
1 tbsp	vegetable oil	15 mL
2 tbsps	caraway seeds	25 mL
2 cups	wholewheat flour	500 mL
3–4 cups	all-purpose flour	750mL–1L
¼ cup	buckwheat flour	50 mL

Stir the water and sugar together in a large warmed mixing bowl. Sprinkle the yeast over the surface and allow to soften and puff for 10 minutes.

Whisk in the sourdough starter, eggs, molasses, honey, salt, vegetable oil and caraway seeds. In a separate bowl, mix the flours together. Add the flour mixture a cupful (250 mL) at a time, beating well after each addition. When it becomes too difficult to mix with the spoon, use your hands. Turn the dough out onto a floured surface and knead for 5 minutes or until the dough becomes smooth and elastic. Wash the mixing bowl, oil it and return the dough to it. Lightly oil the top of the dough. Cover and let rise in a warm place for about 1½ hours or until doubled in bulk. Punch down and cut the dough into 4 pieces. On a floured surface, shape the dough into loaves and place into well-greased 4½" x 8½" (1.5 L) loaf pans. Cover lightly with a kitchen towel and allow to rise again until doubled. This rising will take another hour. Bake in a preheated 350°F (180°C) oven until golden brown, about 30 minutes.

Makes 4 loaves.

Quatsino Wholewheat Bread

Etta, Matt, Steven and Bruce Martinelli   *Quatsino*

Quatsino is a wild, beautiful lightstation. Wide wooden boardwalks run all over the island, around ancient granite boulders that are dotted with clusters of wildflowers, through a rain forest with 700-year-old cedars and past miniature lily ponds ringed with iris. Salmonberries and blackberries pour over the high embankments onto the rock-strewn shore.

Although the climate is cool and damp, Etta had a magnificent, organically grown vegetable garden: four-foot-high Russian kale and many of its brassica cousins, garlic, onions, variegated thyme, pungent oregano, an odd sort of fuzzy mint, calendula that "just keep popping up," a splashy multitude of geraniums, some marginally successful fruit trees ("we just don't get enough light"), potatoes, a greenhouse full of pendulous tomatoes and, of course, a glut of zucchini.

The air at Quatsino is pristine and nearly germ-free. Environment-based allergies are very rare because there is simply no pollution. So when the children of the lights have visitors, or go ashore for school, they catch every contagious disease they meet.

Etta bakes so much bread that she buys the same brand of yeast that most bakeries use. Fermipan is an economical and dependable yeast, and best of all, it works faster and you can use a little less than called for in most recipes.

Because of the yeast, this wholewheat bread is much lighter than most wholegrain breads, yet it has a rich nutty taste. This is a "work crew" sized batch. If you are not having a large group of hungry men over for lunch, freeze any extra loaves in plastic bags — they will keep well for several weeks.

2–3 cups	leftover 7–grain or Red River cereal	500–750 mL
1 cup	skim milk powder	250 mL
1 cup	soy flour	250 mL
2	eggs, beaten	2
½ cup	Barbados molasses	125 mL
2 cups	sourdough starter (p. 69)	500 mL
8 cups	very warm water	2 L
6 cups	unbleached white flour	1.5 L
3 tbsps	Fermipan yeast	45 mL
1 tbsp	lemon juice	15 mL
½ cup	vegetable oil	125 mL
1 tbsp	salt	15 mL
15 cups	wholewheat flour	3.75 L

In a large kettle or commercial style bread mixer, combine the cereal, skim milk powder, soy flour, eggs, molasses and sourdough. Beat in the warm water gradually. Add enough white flour to make a mixture with a sloppy, almost mud-like consistency. Add the yeast and mix well. Let rest for 30–45 minutes.

Beat in the oil, lemon juice and salt.

Add the wholewheat flour, a cupful (250 mL) at a time, until the dough comes away from the sides of the kettle or stops sticking to your hands. Cover and let it rise until it has doubled in bulk, 1½–2 hours. If you are busy, punch it down and let it rise again...it only will make the bread lighter. Turn it out onto a floured surface, knead briefly before shaping into loaves. Place into well-greased 9″ x 5″ (3 L) loaf pans. Etta makes her loaves to fit halfway up in the pans and bakes them when the dough reaches the tops of the pans. Place rolls on greased baking sheets about 2″ (5 cm) apart. Let them rise until doubled. Preheat the oven to 450°F (230°C), put the bread in and reduce the heat immediately to 350°F (180°C). Bake for 1 hour or until deeply golden. Rolls will only need 30 minutes of baking time.

Makes 6 loaves of bread and 3 dozen rolls.

Karen's Not So Basic Bread

Karen and John Coldwell　　　　　　　　　　　　　　　　　*McInnes Island*

The west coast gets into your blood. It's very difficult, if not impossible, to be content away from it once you've spent any time there. Most of the keepers have grown up on the sea and many have roots there that can be traced back several generations. When the Coldwells were working at beautiful Pachena Point, Karen walked the trail where her grandfather had laid the telephone lines decades before.

6 cups	water	1.5 L
½ cup	honey	125 mL
2 tbsps	salt	25 mL
½ cup	vegetable oil	125 mL
1 cup	lukewarm water	250 mL
2 tsps	granulated sugar	10 mL
3 tbsps	active dry yeast	45 mL
1 cup	unground wheat or multi-grained cereal such as Red River or Sunny Boy	250 mL
7 cups	wholewheat flour	1.75 L
10 cups	all-purpose flour	2.5 L

Combine the 6 cups (1.5 L) of the water, honey, salt and oil in a saucepan and heat until lukewarm. Meanwhile, in a large bowl, stir the l cup (250 mL) lukewarm water, granulated sugar and yeast. Set aside and allow to puff for 10 minutes.

Grind the wheat in a blender until the kernels are broken slightly. Karen says that this gives the bread a bit of a "crunch," so don't grind the kernels too fine. Combine the wheat with the wholewheat and all-purpose flours.

Stir the lukewarm mixture into the yeast puff. Add 6 cups (1.5 L) of the flour mixture, beating for 2 minutes. Stir in the rest of the flour mixture with a wooden spoon, 6 cups (1.5 L) at a time, mixing well after each addition. Turn out onto a floured board and knead until the dough is smooth and small bubbles appear on the surface, about 5–7 minutes. Return to a well-greased bowl and oil the top surface. Cover with a kitchen towel and let rise in a warm place until doubled, about 1½ hours. Punch down and turn the dough out onto a floured surface. Cover and let it stand for 20 minutes. Punch down and divide into 6 pieces. Shape into loaves and place into greased 9″ x 5″ (2 L) loaf pans. Cover and let rise again until doubled. This rising should take only about 1 hour. Preheat the oven to 400°F (200°C). Bake the bread for 25–30 minutes. Remove from the pans and let cool. Makes 6 wonderfully crusty loaves.

Wholewheat Broccoli Bread

Judy and Stan Westhaver   *Egg Island*

The work crew grimaced when they were told what they had just devoured—broccoli, YECH! Judy and I giggled all the time we served them.

1½ cups	milk	375 mL
½ cup	fancy molasses	125 mL
1 tbsp	salt	15 mL
½ cup	softened shortening	125 mL
2 cups	water left over from cooking broccoli	500 mL
2 tsps	granulated sugar	10 mL
1 cup	lukewarm water	250 mL
2 tbsps	active dry yeast	25 mL
6 cups	wholewheat flour	1.5 L
4–5 cups	all purpose flour	1–1.25 L

Warm the milk and add the molasses, salt and shortening, stirring until the shortening melts. Add the broccoli water and allow to cool to lukewarm.

Meanwhile, dissolve the sugar in the lukewarm water and sprinkle with the yeast. Let puff for about 10 minutes. With a whisk, stir the yeast mixture and add it to the lukewarm milk. Gradually beat in the wholewheat flour and then add the all-purpose flour a cupful (250 mL) at a time until you have to work the last bit in by hand.

Turn out onto a floured surface and knead for 7–10 minutes. Shape into a ball and place in a well-greased bowl. Oil the top of the dough, cover and let rise in a warm place until doubled, about 1½ hours. Cut into 4 pieces and shape into loaves. Place in well-greased loaf pans. Let rise again until doubled. Bake in a preheated 400°F (200°C) oven until golden or for approximately 30–35 minutes.

Makes 4 loaves.

Stan's Compost Bread

Judy and Stan Westhaver   *Egg Island*

Stan Jr. named this unusual batter bread for the many odds and ends in it.

3 cups	all-purpose flour	750 mL
1 tbsp	active dry yeast	15 mL
2 tsps	salt	10 mL
1¼ cups	warm water	300 mL
¼ cup	molasses	50 mL
2 tbsps	vegetable oil	25 mL

1	egg	1
1 cup	wheat germ	250 mL
1 cup	coarsely grated carrot	250 mL
¼ cup	snipped parsley	50 mL

In a large mixing bowl, combine 2 cups (500 mL) of the flour, the yeast and the salt. Add the water, molasses, oil and egg. Beat at low speed for 30 seconds, scraping the sides. Beat 3 minutes at high speed. Beat in the remaining flour, wheat germ, carrot and parsley. You may have to use a wooden spoon at this point unless you have a powerful mixer. Turn the batter into a well-greased 2 quart (2 L) casserole. Cover and let rise in a warm place until nearly doubled.

Bake for 50–60 minutes in a *preheated* 350°F (180°C) oven, covering with foil after the first 20 minutes. Brush with melted butter if desired. Serve warm, fresh from the oven.

Makes one loaf.

Miso Bread

Lee Wehrwein-Gilbert and John Gilbert, Matthew, Sasha and Oban   *Ballenas Island*

This bread is a macrobiotic version of pumpernickel. Dense, heavy and moist, it slices to almost paper thinness and has a salty, nutty flavor.

Purchase miso at your local health food store. It comes in many forms and flavours, but barley miso is the mildest and most widely available.

¼ cup	barley miso	50 mL
1½ cups	water	375 mL
4 cups	wholewheat flour	1 L

Dissolve the miso in the water. Measure the flour into a mixing bowl and add the miso/water mixture. Stir until thoroughly combined. Turn the dough out onto a well-floured surface and knead for no less than 10 minutes, adding flour as needed. Shape into a small loaf.

Place the loaf into a well-oiled 8½" x 4½" (1.5 L) loaf pan. Brush the surface of the dough with oil, cover with plastic wrap and allow to rise in a warm place overnight. The bread rises very little.

Place in a cold oven and bake at 350°F (180°C) for 1 hour. Set a pan of water on the lower oven rack to ensure even baking.

Loosen the bread and cool before slicing.

Makes one 8½" x 4½" (1.5 L) loaf.

Judy's Better Butter

Judy, Gorden and Guthrie Schweers   *Ivory Island*

This butter remains soft and perfect for spreading even in the refrigerator. With half the cholesterol of regular butter, it still has that wonderful taste. Unfortunately it is not great for cooking and baking.

1 cup	softened butter	250 mL
1 cup	safflower oil	250 mL
¼ cup	skim milk powder	50 mL
2 tbsps	water	25 mL

With an electric mixer, cream the butter. Add the oil, milk powder and water. Continue to beat until light and fluffy. Pour into a covered container and refrigerate.

Makes 2 cups (500 mL).

Crunchy Bread Sticks

Darlene, Allan, Walter and Athena Tansky   *Scarlett Point*

Scarlett Point Lightstation is as beautiful as its name. Hummingbirds flit, a dozen at a time, to the Tanskys' feeder. Deer roam wild and often raid the garden which now has a high white picket fence. A wide salt-water lagoon, once known to the Indians as "Home of the Devil fish," fills and empties with the tides, leaving mussels and limpets exposed for the picking.

Darlene says that these bread sticks are "great with soup," and they are!

1 cup	lukewarm water	250 mL
1 tbsp	granulated sugar	15 mL
1 tbsp	active dry yeast	15 mL
3 cups	all-purpose flour	750 mL
1 tsp	salt	5 mL
1 tbsp	softened shortening	15 mL
1	egg, beaten	1
½ cup	sesame or poppy seeds	125 mL

In a large bowl, combine the water and sugar, stirring to dissolve. Sprinkle with the yeast and allow it to puff for 10 minutes. Stir in the flour, salt and shortening. Turn out onto a lightly floured work surface and knead for 2–3 minutes. Wash the bowl, grease it and return the dough to it. Cover and let rise for 45 minutes. Punch the dough down. Pull off small chunks and, on a floured surface, roll each piece until it is about the thickness of a pencil. Place side by side on a well-greased baking sheet. Brush with beaten egg and sprinkle with sesame or poppy seeds. Allow to rise for 15 minutes. Bake in a preheated 425°F (220°C) oven for 10 minutes.

Makes 3–4 dozen.

Entrance Island Air Buns

Karen, John, Rod and Daniel Chungranes   *Entrance Island*

These rolls have a wonderful homemade flavour — yeasty and just perfect with a good slathering of butter. If you are in a hurry, omit the second rising of the dough, it just makes the buns a little lighter.

3½ cups	lukewarm water	875 mL
⅓ cup	granulated sugar	75 mL
2 tbsps	active dry yeast	25 mL
1½ tbsps	salt	20 mL
1 tbsp	white vinegar	15 mL
2 tbsps	vegetable oil	25 mL
7½–8 cups	all-purpose flour	1.875–2L

In a large mixing bowl, stir together ½ cup (125 mL) of the warm water with 1 tbsp (15 mL) of the sugar. Sprinkle with the yeast and allow it to stand for 10 minutes or until puffed. Measure in the remaining water, sugar, salt, vinegar and oil, stirring until well blended. With a wooden spoon, beat in 4 cups (1 L) of the flour to create a smooth batter. Gradually add the rest of the flour, a cupful (250 mL) at a time, until the dough becomes too difficult to mix with a spoon. Turn the dough out onto a floured work surface and knead in the remaining flour until it becomes smooth and elastic, about 5–7 minutes. Place in a well-greased bowl, rotating the dough to coat all sides. Cover with a kitchen towel and allow it to rise in a warm place until doubled in bulk, about 1½–2 hours. Punch it down and allow it to rise a second time until double — this time should only take about 1 hour. Punch it down and shape into balls about 1½" (4 cm) in diameter. Place 3–4" (7.5–10 cm) apart on a greased baking sheet. Or place them in well-greased muffin tins. Cover and allow to rise until doubled. Bake in a preheated 375°F (190°C) oven for 20–25 minutes or until golden. If you would like a shiny glaze, brush the buns with a mixture of ¼ cup (50 mL) milk and 2 tbsps (25 mL) granulated sugar, about halfway through baking.

Makes 3–4 dozen rolls.

Overnight Crescent Rolls

Judy and Stan Westhaver   *Egg Island*

Stan laughs as he says that "the winds always blow from the northwest, except when they blow from every other direction." Life is certainly like that on the lights of northern BC—swirling, ever-changing winds and more often than not, sheets of rain.

Coming inside after "doing the weathers," I can't imagine a more welcome aroma wafting out of the kitchen than that of these rich and buttery rolls.

1 tbsp	active dry yeast	15 mL
1 cup	warm milk	250 mL
¾ cup	melted butter	175 mL
½ tsp	salt	2 mL
¼ cup	granulated sugar	50 mL
2	eggs, beaten	2
4 cups	all-purpose flour	1 L

In a large warmed mixing bowl, dissolve the yeast in the warm milk, allowing it to stand for 10 minutes or until it begins to puff. Whisk in the butter, salt, sugar and eggs. Measure in the flour, a cupful (250 mL) at a time, beating well after each addition. Turn the dough out onto a lightly floured surface and knead for 3 minutes. Wash the bowl, grease it and return the dough to it. Cover tightly with plastic wrap and refrigerate overnight.

Remove from the refrigerator about 2½–3 hours before baking. Divide the dough into 4 parts and, on a floured surface, roll each into a circle ½" (1 cm) thick. Cut each circle into 12 pie-shaped pieces. Roll each wedge from the wide end to the point. Place the crescents onto an ungreased baking sheet. Cover lightly with a kitchen towel and let rise in a warm place for 1½–2 hours or until doubled. Bake in a preheated 350°F (180°C) oven for 10–15 minutes.

Makes 4 dozen.

Christmas Brioche

Lina, Jean, Isabelle and François Beaudet   *Bonilla Island*

Loaded into a heavy workboat, I had to lick my lips to determine whether it was rain or salt spray lashing my face. When I jumped ashore on Bonilla Island, I was greeted by Jean and Lina Beaudet from Huberdeau, Quebec. With their little family, they are a pocket of French Canadian customs and foodways on the edge of the Pacific Ocean. Lina admits that like any family in relative isolation, they have to work hard at putting the meaning into the celebration. They celebrate mass early on Christmas Eve so that it coincides with the exact moment that their relatives are in church "back home." She bakes this brioche only once a year, for Christmas morning breakfast...that way it remains a special French tradition on the lights.

1 cup	milk	250 mL
½ cup	granulated sugar	125 mL
2 tsps	salt	10 mL
½ cup	softened shortening	125 mL
¾ cup	cold water	175 mL
½ cup	lukewarm water	125 mL
2 tsps	granulated sugar	10 mL
2 tbsps	active dry yeast	25 mL
2	eggs, beaten	2
6–6½ cups	all-purpose flour	1250–1625 mL

In a heavy saucepan, warm the milk. Stir in the sugar, salt and shortening until dissolved. Measure in the cold water and cool until barely warm.

In a large bowl, combine the ½ cup (125 mL) lukewarm water with the 2 teaspoons (10 mL) sugar. Sprinkle with the yeast and set aside for 10 minutes to puff. Mix well before adding to the milk mixture. Whisk in the eggs and 3½ cups (875 mL) of the flour. Beat well until the batter is soft and elastic.

Add the remaining flour, a cupful (250 mL) at a time, beating well after each addition. Scrape out onto a floured surface and knead for 5–7 minutes. The dough will be smooth and satiny. Place the dough back into a greased bowl, oil the top and cover with waxed paper and a kitchen towel. Let it rise in a warm place until doubled, about 1½ hours. Punch it down and turn out onto a floured surface. Cut into two and roll each piece into a long, narrow rectangle about 24" x 8" (60 cm x 20 cm). Combine the following ingredients and spread half the filling on each brioche:

¼ cup	soft butter	50 mL
1 cup	brown sugar	250 mL
2 tsps	cinnamon	10 mL
1 cup	raisins	250 mL

Roll up, jelly-roll fashion and pinch the edges to seal them. Twist each piece into a circle and lay them on well-greased baking sheets. Slash the tops a few times with a sharp knife. Cover and allow them to rise until doubled, about another 1½ hours.

Bake in a preheated 350°F (180°C) oven until golden, about 35 minutes.

While the brioche is still warm cover it with the following icing:

2 tbsps	softened butter	25 mL
1½ cups	icing sugar	375 mL
¼ tsp	vanilla	1 mL
2 tbsps	apple juice	25 mL

Beat together and spread over the warm bread. Decorate with slivered almonds and glazed red and green cherry halves.

Makes 2 brioche.

Crescent Rolls

This recipe also makes lovely, delicate crescent rolls. Cut the dough into 4 pieces and roll each piece into a circle about 9″ (22 cm) across. Cut into 8 pie-shaped wedges. Spread with softened butter if you wish and perhaps a few poppy seeds. Roll each piece from the wide end and shape into crescents. Place on a well-greased baking sheet. Let rise until doubled before baking in a preheated 350°F (180°C) oven for 10–15 minutes.

Makes 32 rolls.

Currant Bread

Kathleen and Don Richards   *Merry Island*

When I sloshed ashore at Lucy Island the assistant keeper and his family greeted me. They were a little lonely, having just said goodbye to their friends, the Richardses, who transferred to Merry Island in the "southern agency." This is their all-time favourite bread recipe, one that keeps and in fact improves over 2 or 3 days. Slice into thick slabs and serve with "mega-butter."

2 tbsps	active dry yeast	25 mL
½ cup	lukewarm water	125 mL
2 cups	milk, scalded	500 mL
1½ tsps	salt	7 mL
1 cup	granulated sugar	250 mL
1 cup	softened shortening	250 mL
9 cups	all purpose flour	2.25 L
6	eggs, beaten	6
1½ cups	currants	375 mL

Soften the yeast in the lukewarm water. Add the hot milk to the salt, sugar and shortening, stirring to dissolve the sugar and melt the shortening. When lukewarm, beat in the yeast and half the flour. Cover and let rise in a warm place until light and puffy, about 1 hour.

Add the eggs, currants and remaining flour, mixing by hand when necessary. Turn out onto a floured surface and knead for 4–5 minutes. The dough will be smooth and elastic. Place in a greased bowl, oil the surface of the dough, cover and let rise in a warm place until doubled, about 1½ hours.

Punch down, divide and shape into 3 loaves. Place in greased 9″ x 5″ (2 L) loaf pans. Cover and let rise until double again. Bake in a preheated 350°F (180°C) oven for 30–40 minutes or until deep golden brown. Remove from the pans and cool completely before storing.

Makes 3 loaves.

Portuguese Sweet Bread

Dan and Fil McMurray   *Pointer Island (now automated)*

Fil's parents are from Portugal, and her skill in creating yeast breads reflects that heritage. This is a lovely Eastertime treat, full of eggs, candied fruit and nuts.

2 tbsps	active dry yeast	25 mL
½ cup	very warm water	125 mL
1 cup	milk	250 mL
½ cup	butter	125 mL
2 tsps	salt	10 mL
6	eggs, at room temperature	6
1½ cups	granulated sugar	375 mL
7½–8½ cups	all-purpose flour	1875–2125 mL
1–1½ cups	raisins	250–375 mL
1–1½ cups	walnuts	250–375 mL
7½–8½ cups	all purpose flour	1875–2125 mL

Sprinkle the yeast over the warm water in a large mixing bowl. Set aside. Scald the milk in a saucepan over medium heat. Stir in the butter and salt. Cool to lukewarm.

Meanwhile, whisk the eggs and sugar together, beating until light. Add the milk mixture to the eggs and combine with the yeast. Gradually beat in 3 cups (750 mL) of the flour with a wooden spoon. Mix in the raisins and nuts. Continue to add the flour, a cupful (250 mL) at a time, mixing well after each addition.

Turn the dough out onto a floured surface and knead until smooth, about 8–10 minutes, adding flour as necessary. Place in a greased mixing bowl, turning the dough to grease the top. Cover with plastic wrap and let rise until doubled, about 1½–2 hours.

Punch down and let rest 10 minutes. Cut into 3 equal pieces and shape each into a smooth ball. flatten into 8–9″ (20–22 cm) rounds. Press into 3 greased 9″ (22 cm) cake pans. Cover with a kitchen towel and let rise until doubled in bulk.

Bake in a preheated 350°F (180°C) oven for 30 minutes or until well browned. Brush with melted butter while hot. Cool before slicing...if you can wait (I couldn't).

Makes three 9″ (22 cm) loaves.

Bacon and Maple Buns

Gwen and Doug Fraser   *Pine Island*

Gwen's expertise in bread baking really shines through in this recipe. It's almost enough to make me take up helicopter flying so that I could just drop in at Pine every day or so.

3¾–4½ cups	all-purpose flour	925–1125 mL
1 tbsp	active dry yeast	15 mL
½ cup	granulated sugar	125 mL
1¼ cups	milk	300 mL
½ cup	butter	125 mL
1 tsp	salt	5 mL
1	egg	1
¾ cup	butter, melted	175 mL
⅔ cup	brown sugar, packed	150 mL
¼ tsp	maple flavouring	1 ml
½ lb	side bacon, crisply cooked, drained and crushed	225 g

In a mixing bowl, combine 1½ cups (375 mL) of the flour, the undissolved yeast and ¼ cup (50 mL) of the sugar. Heat the milk, ½ cup (125 mL) butter, the remaining granulated sugar and salt in a saucepan until the butter almost melts. Add to the dry ingredients in the mixing bowl. Break in the egg and beat at low speed for about 30 seconds, scraping the sides of the bowl constantly. Increase the speed to high and beat for 3 minutes. By hand, stir in enough of the remaining flour to make a moderately stiff dough. Turn out onto a floured surface and knead until smooth and elastic, about 5–7 minutes.

Place the dough into a well-greased bowl, turning once to grease the surface of the dough. Cover and let rise until doubled in bulk, about 1½ hours.

Meanwhile, combine the ¾ cup (175 mL) melted butter, brown sugar and maple flavouring. Divide it evenly among 24 muffin tins.

Punch the dough down, dividing in half. Cover and let rest for 10 minutes. On a floured surface, roll each half of the dough to a 12" x 8" (30 x 20 cm) rectangle. Sprinkle with bacon. Roll up, jelly-roll fashion, beginning with the longest side. Cut each section of dough into 12 pieces and place, cut side down, into the prepared muffin tins. Cover and let rise until doubled, about 25–30 minutes.

Bake in a preheated 350°F (180°C) oven for 20–25 minutes. Loosen the edges and invert onto racks to cool.

Makes two dozen buns.

Spicy Hot Cross Buns

Wendy, Jim, Jessie and Melissa Abram   *Cape Mudge*

Up the Inside Passage near Campbell River, the Cape Mudge lightstation watches over thousands of sport fishermen each summer when the World Salmon Fishing Championship is held there. The fishermen go to test their luck at catching the famous tyee salmon, any big spring *(Oncorhynchus tshawytscha)* over 13 kilograms. Every so often a boat is swamped by the wind which literally funnels down Dixon Passage. Then the keepers, who maintain a constant vigil by their huge picture window during a gusty day, start the rescue operation. Jim says that in their quest for the Big One, many fishermen take unnecessary risks that lead them into life-threatening danger.

½ cup	warm water	125 mL
⅓ cup	granulated sugar	75 mL
2 tbsps	active dry yeast	25 mL
⅓ cup	milk	75 mL
3¾ cups	all-purpose flour	925 mL
2 tsps	cinnamon	10 mL
½ tsp	ground cloves	2 mL
½ tsp	allspice	2 mL
½ cup	vegetable oil	125 mL
3	eggs, well beaten	3
1 cup	raisins or currants	250 mL

Stir the warm water and 1 tsp (5 mL) of the sugar together in a large mixing bowl. Sprinkle with the yeast and allow the mixture to puff for 10 minutes.

Beat in the remaining sugar, the milk, 1 cup (250 mL) of the flour and the spices. Whisk in the oil and the eggs thoroughly.

Stir in the remaining flour, a cupful (250 mL) at a time. Add the raisins or currants. Gather the dough up into a ball and turn out onto a lightly floured board. Knead gently for 4–5 minutes.

Wash and grease the mixing bowl. Return the dough to it and cover with a kitchen towel. Allow the dough to rise for 45–60 minutes, or until doubled in bulk. Punch the dough down and knead it again on a floured surface for a minute. Divide the dough into 18 pieces, shape into small buns and place on a greased cookie sheet. Cover and let rise again until doubled, about 45 minutes. With scissors, snip the top of each bun in the shape of a cross. Bake for 12–15 minutes in a preheated 350°F (160°C) oven. After baking, brush with a little melted butter.

Makes 18 fragrant buns.

Walnut Orange Stickies

Gwen and Doug Fraser   *Pine Island*

These sweet, yeasty treats taste as yummy as they sound!

Sweet Dough

1 cup	milk	250 mL
¼ cup	granulated sugar	50 mL
¾ tsp	salt	4 mL
2 tbsps	shortening	25 mL
1 tbsp	active dry yeast	15 mL
¼ cup	very warm water	50 mL
1	egg, beaten	1
3–3½ cups	all-purpose flour	750–875 mL

Filling

¼ cup	melted butter or margarine	50 mL
¼ cup	granulated sugar	50 mL
1 tsp	cinnamon	5 mL

Topping

¾ cup	granulated sugar	175 mL
¾ cup	water	175 mL
1 tsp	cinnamon	5 ml

1 tsp	grated orange rind	5 mL
⅛ tsp	salt	.5 mL
1 cup	chopped walnuts	250 mL

Prepare the dough by heating the milk, sugar, salt and shortening in a small saucepan. When the shortening is melted remove from the heat and cool to lukewarm. In a separate bowl, sprinkle the yeast over the warm water, stirring until dissolved. Add the cooled milk mixture. Beat in the egg and about 2 cups (500 mL) of the flour until the batter becomes smooth. Mix in the remaining flour to create a stiff dough. Turn out onto a floured surface and knead for 8–10 minutes. Place in a greased bowl, oil the surface of the dough and cover with a kitchen towel. Let rise in a warm place for about one hour or until doubled.

While the dough is rising, make the filling by stirring together the melted butter, sugar and cinnamon. Set aside.

Prepare the topping by combining the sugar, water, cinnamon, orange rind and salt in a medium-sized saucepan. Heat, stirring constantly, to boiling. Cook over medium heat for 10 minutes, or until thick and syrupy. Pour half the syrup into a greased 8″ (20 cm) or 9″ (22 cm) cake pan. Sprinkle evenly with the walnuts and set aside.

Punch the dough down and turn out onto a floured surface. Roll out into a rectangle about 12″ x 16″ (30 x 40 cm). Spread generously with the filling. Beginning at the long end, roll the dough to enclose the filling. With a sharp knife, cut into 16 slices. Place, cut side down, into the baking pan. Cover with a kitchen towel and let rise until doubled.

Pour the remaining syrup over the rolls and bake in a preheated 350°F (180°C) oven for 15 minutes or until they are glazed and brown. Cool in the pan, on a wire rack, for 5 minutes. Loosen the edges and invert onto a serving plate. Serve warm.

Makes 16 sticky buns.

Traditional Raised Doughnuts

Gwen and Doug Fraser   *Pine Island*

Fry doughnuts in a heavy, high-sided saucepan and always use a thermometer to gauge the temperature correctly. I use chopsticks to flip them and lift them out easily.

Gwen says that these are the best doughnuts she has ever made, but cautions, with a smile, that they must be eaten right away or they will become stale—or that's what her kids tell her.

1 tbsp	active dry yeast	15 mL
1 cup	lukewarm water	250 mL
¼ cup	granulated sugar	50 mL
1 tsp	salt	5 ml
¼ cup	melted shortening	50 mL
1	egg, beaten	1
3½–4 cups	all-purpose flour	.875–1 L
	vegetable oil for frying, as needed	

Sprinkle the yeast over ¼ cup (50 mL) of the warm water, stirring to dissolve. Add the remaining water, sugar, salt and melted shortening, mixing well. Beat in the egg and 1 cup (250 mL) of the flour. Combine the batter thoroughly. Measure in the remaining flour, working in the last flour by hand if necessary. Turn out onto a floured board and knead for 5–10 minutes. Place the dough into a greased bowl, turning it to cover all sides of the dough with shortening. Cover with a kitchen towel and let rise until doubled. Turn out onto a floured surface and roll out to ½–¾" (1–2 cm) thickness. Cut into doughnut shapes and place on greased cookie sheets. The small doughnut holes may either be re-worked into the dough or set aside to rise themselves. When doubled, in about 1 hour, fry in deep fat at 350–375°F (175–190°C). Drain on paper towelling and dip hot doughnuts into a glaze made with a little icing sugar, vanilla and milk. Cool on racks.

Makes about 2 dozen doughnuts.

Muffins for Breakfast, Biscuits for Dinner and Coffeecakes for the Helicopter Pilots

Race Rocks

Joan Redhead's Popular Muffins

Joan and Charles Redhead   *Race Rocks*

The most exotic undersea life is often found in areas of wild and uncontrolled currents. It then goes without saying that if you are a scuba diver, Race Rocks is an underwater dream. The students of nearby Pearson College, one of the world's international colleges, have been appointed the wardens of this magnificent marine preserve. Slipping amongst the wide kelp ribbons, arcing downwards to investigate a hidden undersea wall of spiny red sea urchins or buddying up with a seal, I found my dreams of flying came true.

With the old adrenalin pumping, I surged with the tide through undersea forests to finally pull myself out of the ocean at the dock where the dive boat was tied up. Joan had just ferried in from a shopping trip to Victoria and immediately she and Charles insisted that our dive team join them for tea and these incredible and justifiably famous muffins. She has been known to bake up to 600 a day for her special young friends at Pearson College.

4	eggs	4
1½ cups	vegetable oil	375 mL
1¾ cups	granulated sugar	425 mL
3 cups	all-purpose flour	750 mL
2½ tsps	baking powder	12 mL
1½ tsps	baking soda	7 mL
¾ tsp	salt	4 mL

Applesauce Variation

2 tsps	cinnamon	10 mL
2 cups	applesauce	500 mL

Zucchini/Pineapple or Carrot/Pineapple Variation

1½ tsps	cinnamon	7 mL
¾ tsp	freshly grated nutmeg	4 mL
1½ cups	grated carrot or zucchini	375 mL
1 14 oz tin	crushed pineapple, well drained	1 398 mL tin

Preheat the oven to 350°F (180°C).

In a large mixing bowl, beat together the eggs, oil and sugar. In a separate bowl, combine the flour, baking powder, baking soda, salt and spices with a fork. Add the dry ingredients to the creamed mixture alternately with either the applesauce or the carrot/zucchini and pineapple. Spoon into well-greased muffin tins and bake for 15–20 minutes. Cool the muffins for 5 minutes before removing from the pans.

Makes 2 dozen large muffins.

Cape Mudge

Best Ever Bran Muffins

Wendy, Jim, Jessie and Melissa Abram   *Cape Mudge*

It's funny how good recipes travel. This is almost identical to one that won several ribbons in our local fall fair. It really is a prize winner!

2¾ cups	all-purpose flour	675 mL
2 tsps	baking powder	10 mL
1 cup	soft butter or margarine	250 mL
2 cups	brown sugar	500 mL
2 tbsps	molasses	25 mL
¼ tsp	salt	1 mL
1½ cups	natural bran	375 mL
1 cup	walnuts	250 mL
1½ cups	raisins	375 mL
2 tsps	baking soda	10 mL
2 cups	sour milk or buttermilk	500 mL
2	eggs, well beaten	2

Preheat the oven to 375°F (190°C).

Sift the flour with the baking powder. Set aside. Cream the butter and sugar in a large bowl. Add the molasses, salt, bran and the flour mixture. Stir in the walnuts and raisins. In a separate bowl, whisk the soda, sour milk and eggs together. Pour into the first mixture, stirring until barely combined. Spoon the batter into well-greased muffin tins. Bake for 20–25 minutes.

Makes 18 muffins.

Blueberry Bran Muffins

Gwen and Doug Fraser   *Pine Island*

Before visiting Pine Island, Pen Brown of the Coast Guard Base in Victoria raved about the quality of the Frasers' stone work. It is superb—low walls follow walkways and outline perfectly groomed gardens.

⅓ cup	softened butter	75 mL
½ cup	granulated sugar	125 mL
1	egg	1
¾ cup	milk	175 mL
1/4 tsp	vanilla	1 mL
1⅔ cups plus 1 tbsp	all-purpose flour	415 mL
2½ tsps	baking powder	12 mL
½ tsp	salt	2 mL
¼ cup	natural bran	50 mL
1¼ cups	fresh blueberries or frozen blueberries, slightly thawed	300 mL

Preheat the oven to 425°F (220°C).

Cream the butter and sugar in a large mixing bowl. Whip in the egg, milk and vanilla, mixing well. Stir the flour, baking powder, salt and bran together. Stir into the creamed mixture until the dry ingredients are moistened. Do not overmix. The batter will not be smooth. Toss the blueberries with the 1 tbsp (15 mL) flour and fold into the batter.

Grease the bottom only of 12 muffin tins. Divide the batter among them until they are about ⅔ full. Bake for 20–25 minutes or until golden. Let stand for 5 minutes before loosening from the pan and serving piping hot.

Makes one dozen.

Cheddar Buttermilk Bran Muffins

Linda and Don Weeden   *Cape Scott*

Try these tangy muffins with a hearty chowder or even a light salad. I like extra small chunks of cheese placed on top of the batter before baking...they melt and become a deep toasted amber.

1½ cups	buttermilk or sour milk	375 mL
1 cup	natural bran	250 mL
¼ cup	softened shortening	50 mL
⅓ cup	granulated sugar	75 mL
1	egg	1

1½ cups	all-purpose flour	375 mL
1½ tsps	baking powder	7 mL
¼ tsp	baking soda	1 mL
½ tsp	salt	2 mL
1 cup	grated sharp cheddar cheese	250 mL
	extra cheddar chunks (optional)	

Preheat the oven to 350°F (180°C).

Stir the bran and buttermilk together and set aside to soak.

Cream the shortening and sugar until fluffy. Add the egg and beat for a few seconds longer. Combine with the bran and buttermilk. Stir the flour, baking powder, baking soda and salt together, then add to the batter. Fold in the grated cheese, mixing only until no dry spots remain. Fill greased or paper-lined muffin tins ⅔ full. Top with additional cheese if desired. Bake for 20–25 minutes.

Makes 12–14 muffins.

Mincemeat Bran Muffins

Darlene, Allan, Walter and Athena Tansky   *Scarlett Point*

Bake this muffin batter immediately or store it for up to 3 weeks in the refrigerator.

2	eggs	2
¾ cup	vegetable oil	175 mL
¾ cup	granulated sugar	175 mL
¼ cup	molasses	50 mL
2 cups	milk	500 mL
1¼ cups	mincemeat	300 mL
1 cup	natural bran	250 mL
2¼ cups	all-purpose flour	550 mL
2 tsps	baking soda	10 ml
2 tsps	baking powder	10 ml

Preheat the oven to 375°F (190°C).

In a large mixing bowl, beat the eggs, oil, sugar, molasses, milk and mincemeat. Stir in the bran and set aside. Combine the flour, baking soda and baking powder. Add the dry ingredients to the first mixture, stirring just to blend. Spoon into well greased or paper-lined muffin tins and bake for 15–18 minutes. Or refrigerate the batter until needed.

Makes about 18 large muffins.

Buttermilk Oatmeal Muffins with Dates

Pauline, Joe and Cindy Balmer   *Estevan Point*

This is one of those great basic recipes that should be in everyone's repertoire. Omit the dates and add raisins, grate in some fresh lemon or orange rind, toss in a handful of chopped nuts, even glazed Christmas fruit is super...!

1 cup	oatmeal	250 mL
1 cup	buttermilk	250 mL
1	egg, beaten	1
½ cup	brown sugar	125 mL
½ cup	melted butter or shortening	125 mL
1 cup	chopped dates	250 mL
1 cup	all-purpose flour	250 mL
1 tsp	baking powder	5 mL
½ tsp	baking soda	2 mL
½ tsp	salt	2 mL

In a large mixing bowl, soak the oatmeal in the buttermilk for 1 hour.

Preheat the oven to 400°F (200°C).

Add the egg and sugar to the oatmeal mixture, beating well. Whisk in the melted butter and dates. In a separate bowl, stir together the flour, baking powder, baking soda and salt. Add all at once to the first bowl, stirring just enough to moisten. Spoon the batter into 12 greased or paper-lined muffin tins. Bake for 20 minutes or until they begin to brown.

Makes 1 dozen.

Mom's Wheat Germ Muffins

Wendy, Jim, Jessie and Melissa Abram   *Cape Mudge*

Knowing that sixteen cougars had just been removed from Quadra Island made our stroll in the brilliant morning sunlight, among the wild Nootka rose bushes, a little more exciting.

This is Wendy's mom's favourite muffin recipe.

1 cup	all-purpose flour	250 mL
1 tbsp	baking powder	15 mL
⅛ tsp	baking soda	.5 mL
½ cup	brown sugar	125 mL
¾ cup	wheat germ	175 mL
½–¾	cup raisins or fresh blueberries	25–175 mL
1	egg	1
¾ cup	milk	175 mL

| ¼ cup | vegetable oil | 50 mL |

Preheat the oven to 375°F (190°C).

In a large mixing bowl, stir together the flour, baking powder, baking soda, brown sugar, wheat germ and raisins. In a separate bowl, whisk together the egg, milk and oil. Make a well in the dry ingredients and pour in the egg mixture all at once. Blend only until there are no dry spots remaining.

Pour the batter into 12 greased or paper-lined muffin tins. Bake for 20–25 minutes or until lightly golden brown. Great with butter and a mild cheese.

Makes 12 muffins.

Egg Island

Cheesey Potato Muffins

Judy and Stan Westhaver   *Egg Island*

There are so many strange stories from the lights that it is impossible to recount them all. But in many of them there is a recurring theme: the inability of people to understand the danger of the Pacific Coast.

The *Thomas Crosby V* is a United Church mission ship which periodically visits most of the remote outposts around the northern part of Vancouver Island up to the Alaska border. The crew was buzzed by a small seaplane when they were en route to one of their stops. The plane landed and the pilot leaned out the window and yelled "Which way is Seattle?" He had no map, no compass and no radio.

The same sort of story is often repeated. Men have set out on their fancy pleasure boats with a service station road map as their only guide. Others limply explain to the disgusted lightkeeper that their "chartbook blew out the window" and would they please point them in the direction of Ketchikan, Alaska. The meaning of the expression "three sheets to the wind" takes on new meaning when a boatload of party-goers dry out enough to realize they are not only lost but in danger of being caught in a storm that can swamp any rescue ship that may attempt to save them. All of these events have been part of Stan and Judy's life on the lights.

1 cup	mashed potato (1 large baking potato)	250 mL
1 cup	milk	250 mL
2 cups	all-purpose flour	500 mL
1 tbsp	baking powder	15 mL
1 tsp	dried dill weed	5 mL
½ tsp	salt	2 mL
⅛ tsp	freshly ground pepper	.5 mL
½ cup	grated Parmesan cheese	125 mL
2 tbsps	grated onion (optional)	25 mL
2	eggs, beaten	2
¼ cup	butter, melted	50 mL

Preheat the oven to 400°F (200°C).

Mash the potato with ¼ cup (50 mL) of the milk. In a large bowl, combine the flour, baking powder, dill weed, salt, pepper and cheese. Whisk together the remaining milk, onion, eggs and butter. Make a well in the centre of the dry ingredients and pour in the milk mixture and the mashed potato, beating until just barely combined. Do not overmix. Divide the batter among 12 greased or paper lined muffin tins. Bake for 25 minutes or until golden brown. Let cool for 5–10 minutes before removing from the pan.

Makes 12 muffins.

Golden Breakfast Corn Cake

Kay and Fred Pratt   *Ballenas Island*

Ballenas was named in 1794 by the captain of a Spanish surveying ship who watched in wonder the huge pods of whales breaking the surface near this particular group of islands.

Kay Pratt, the wife of the senior keeper, says that this version of corn bread should be served warm, cut in half, spread with butter and have maple syrup drizzled all over it. I agree!

¾ cup	corn meal	175 mL
1 cup	all-purpose flour	250 mL
1 tbsp	baking powder	15 mL

⅓ cup	granulated sugar	75 mL
½ tsp	salt	2 mL
1 cup	milk	250 mL
2	eggs, well beaten	2
2 tbsps	vegetable oil	25 mL

Preheat the oven to 400°F (200°C).

Combine the corn meal, flour, baking powder, sugar and salt in a large mixing bowl. Whisk together the milk, eggs and oil. Make a well in the dry ingredients and pour in the milk mixture, stirring to combine completely.

Pour the batter into a well-greased 9″ (22 cm) round cake pan. Bake for 20 minutes or until a testing needle comes out clean.

Great with bacon or ham or fresh preserves or...

Makes 4–6 servings.

Buttermilk Raisin Coffee Cake

Frances Collette   *Merry Island*

This is certainly one of the very best coffee cakes that I have ever tasted.

¾ cup	softened butter	175 mL
1½ cups	brown sugar	375 mL
3	eggs	3
3 cups	all-purpose flour	750 mL
2 tsps	baking powder	10 ml
1 tsp	salt	5 mL
1 tsp	baking soda	5 mL
1 cup	buttermilk	250 mL
1 tbsp	grated orange or lemon rind	15 mL

Streusel Topping

½ cup	brown sugar	125 mL
⅓ cup	all-purpose flour	75 mL
2 tsps	cinnamon	10 mL
¼ cup	softened butter	50 mL
1 cup	raisins	250 mL

Orange Glaze

1 cup	icing sugar	250 mL
2 tbsps	orange juice	25 mL

Preheat the oven to 350°F (180°C).

Cream the butter and sugar until light and fluffy. Add the eggs one at a time, beating after each addition. Stir together the flour, baking powder, salt and baking soda. Add to the creamed mixture alternately with the buttermilk. Stir in the peel.

Grease and flour a 10″ (25 cm) tube pan.

Make the streusel in a separate bowl by combining the sugar, flour and cinnamon. With a fork, blend in the softened butter completely.

Pour half the batter into the prepared pan, spreading evenly. Top with half the streusel and half the raisins. Spread with the remaining batter and sprinkle the rest of the streusel over the top. Bake for 50–60 minutes or until golden. Let stand for 5 minutes before removing from the pan. Turn out onto a cake plate.

Make the glaze by mixing the icing sugar and orange juice. Add the remaining ½ cup (125 mL) raisins. While the coffee cake is cooling, drizzle with the glaze. You'll have to serve it right away, because it is almost impossible to wait until it cools!

Makes one 10″ (25 cm) coffee cake.

Christmas 1982

It was quite a Christmas for the Schweers family. They were all prepared for the festive season when the barometer began to plummet. As the winds rose and the waves began to pound the shoreline more ferociously than for many years, the two lightkeepers became uneasy. Christmas or not, the Pacific never rests. In the early morning the winds were blowing a Force 10 gale with gusts to 60 knots.

All of a sudden a huge wave swept over the station, slicing, tearing, ripping, cutting, smashing. The house was inundated and the kitchen was filled with sea water, flying glass and debris.

A 1000 gallon water tank slid 20 feet before it hit the house and huge boulders scraped the siding from their dwelling and destroyed platforms, stairways and railings. The furnace was smothered and as the water flowed out the basement door down an embankment, the Schweerses pinched themselves to make sure they were still alive. Miraculously, they and their junior keeper, Andy Findlay, were not injured.

The station was a disaster but with the help of their trusty wood stove, the same one that had saved the canoeists at Nootka, they dried out, literally picked up the pieces and, in the true pioneering spirit that is so typical of lightkeepers, stayed on the island.

Cinnamon Wholewheat Popovers

Judy, Gorden and Guthrie Schweers   *Ivory Island*

Try these for breakfast, crispy and delicious with butter melting over them.

3	eggs	3
1 cup	milk	250 mL
1 cup	wholewheat flour	250 mL
3 tbsps	melted butter	45 mL
1 tsp	cinnamon	5 mL
¼ tsp	salt	1 mL
1 tbsp	granulated sugar (optional)	15 mL

Preheat the oven to 400°F (200°C).

Combine all the ingredients in the bowl of a food processor or in a blender. Cover and process for 30 seconds. Fill well-greased muffin tins ⅔ full. Bake for 30 minutes. Prick the tops of the popovers with a sharp knife and return to the oven for an additional 5 to 10 minutes. Serve with butter and wildflower honey or maple syrup.

Makes 1 dozen.

Sourdough Biscuits

Joan and Charles Redhead   *Race Rocks*

Located just southwest of Victoria, Race Rocks was named for the violent rip tides that encase the island in streams of kelp and whirlpools. The currents spelled disaster for many an early mariner. Finally, in 1860, a light was constructed—the second on the BC coast. The actual tower was quarried in Scotland, brought around Cape Horn as ballast and reassembled to guide ships into the soon-to-be-booming port of Victoria.

The Redheads love their life there. They are surrounded constantly by the barking sea lion and seal colonies. Fog often rolls in without notice and the bellowing of the fog horn becomes another voice in the discordant chorus.

1 cup	all-purpose flour	250 mL
2 tsps	baking powder	10 mL
½ tsp	baking soda	2 mL
1/2 tsp	salt	2 mL
1 cup	sourdough starter (p. 69)	250 mL
¼ cup	vegetable oil	50 mL
1 cup	minced onion, cooked ham and/or chunks of cheese	250 mL

Preheat the oven to 400°F (200°C).

Stir together the flour, baking powder, baking soda and salt. Combine the sourdough starter and oil, and add it to the dry ingredients. Gently fold in the onion, ham and/or cheese. Turn out onto a lightly floured surface and knead several times to barely combine. Tear off small lumps of dough and place on a greased baking sheet until they are beginning to brown. These fragrant biscuits are really good with butter melting all over them.

Makes 14–16 biscuits.

Crusty Cheese Biscuits

Gwen and Doug Fraser   *Pine Island*

Gwen suggests these as an excellent base for Eggs Benedict or all by themselves, smothered with butter and homemade jam.

2 cups	all-purpose flour	500 mL
1½ tsps	cream of tartar	7 ml
1 tsp	baking soda	5 mL
1 tsp	salt	5 mL
2 tbsps	brown sugar	25 mL
¼ cup	soft butter or margarine	50 ml
1 cup	coarsely grated sharp cheddar	250 mL
¾–1 cup	milk	175–250 mL

Preheat the oven to 425°F (190°C).

Sift the flour, cream of tartar, baking soda, salt and brown sugar into a large bowl. Cut in the butter until the mixture is crumbly. Stir in the cheese and just enough milk to make the batter thin enough to drop from a spoon. Stir only until the dry ingredients are incorporated.

Cover a large cookie sheet with foil and grease it. Drop 12–14 spoonfuls of batter onto the sheet. Bake for 12–15 minutes or until beginning to turn golden. Serve hot from the oven.

Makes 12–14 biscuits.

Cheddar Onion Biscuits

Kay and Fred Pratt   *Ballenas Island*

Skimming into Ballenas at a much lower altitude than usual (I think we were staying out of harm's way), we were constantly aware of the military presence close by at Nanoose Bay, a major torpedo testing range. We made sure that the position of our speedy little helicopter was well and duly noted.

3	green onions, minced	3
¾ cup	grated cheddar cheese	175 mL
2 cups	all-purpose flour	500 mL
2 tbsps	granulated sugar	25 mL
2 tbsps	baking powder	25 mL
½ tsp	salt	2 mL
⅓ cup	shortening	75 mL
1 cup	milk	250 mL

Preheat the oven to 400°F (200°C).

Combine the onions and cheese in a large mixing bowl. Measure in the flour, sugar, baking powder and salt, stirring thoroughly with a fork. Cut in the shortening with a pastry blender until the mixture has the appearance of fine crumbs. Add the milk, ½ cup (125 mL) at a time, mixing gently after each addition.

Turn the dough onto a floured board and knead lightly until it just begins to hold together. Pat or roll out with a floured rolling pin to approximately 1" (2.5 cm) thick. Cut with a small glass dipped in flour, and place on a well-greased baking sheet. Let the biscuits rest for 5 minutes before popping them into the oven for 12–15 minutes or until just beginning to brown.

Makes 10–12 biscuits depending on the size of your glass.

Old-Fashioned Lemon Loaf

Gwen and Doug Fraser   *Pine Island*

It was over seven years before the Frasers met any other lightkeepers. They had spoken often over the radio-telephone, but had never stood face to face with their co-workers. Since then they have had fleeting exchanges at Coast Guard-sponsored courses, but personal contact is still very infrequent.

1 cup	granulated sugar	250 mL
½ cup	softened butter	125 mL
2	eggs, beaten	2
½ cup	milk	125 mL
1½ cups	all-purpose flour	375 mL
1 tsp	baking powder	5 mL
1 tsp	salt	5 mL
1 tsp	grated lemon rind	5 mL

Glaze

| 2 tbsps | fresh lemon juice | 25 mL |
| ¼ cup | granulated sugar | 50 ml |

Preheat the oven to 350°F (180°C).

In a large mixing bowl, cream the sugar and butter. Add the eggs, beating constantly, until light and fluffy. Whip in the milk. In a separate bowl, stir together the flour, baking powder and salt. Fold into the creamed mixture along with the lemon rind.

Grease and line a 9″ x 5″ (2 L) loaf pan with waxed paper. Spread the batter evenly in the baking pan. Bake for 45–60 minutes or until a testing needle comes out clean. Remove from the oven and while the loaf is still in the pan, stir the lemon juice and sugar together and drizzle the glaze over the loaf. Let cool before removing from the pan.

Makes one 9″ x 5″ (2 L) loaf.

A Dozen Cakes

Merry Island

Mabel the Duck's Cake

Betty and Rex Pendril ("Pen") Brown   *Formerly of Pine Island*

Pen Brown is really Santa Claus in disguise. For 364 days, he doubles as a gregarious gentleman at the Victoria Coast Guard Base who is in charge of aids to navigation and lots of general public relations. But underneath his civilian clothes lurks St. Nick, all ready to jump aboard the *George R. Pearkes* and bring Christmas via icebreaker and helicopter to the children of the west coast lights. The weather has never stopped him, even gales that ripped fences down in Victoria. (Did you know that's where Santa really lives? At his venerable age why should he live at the North Pole when he can grow kiwi fruit in his own back yard?)

The tradition of the "Santa Claus run" began in the early 1960s when George Thomas, a steward of the ship *Camsel* saw how isolated the children of the lights were. It seemed that the spirit of Christmas flowed in the veins of that crew and, using funds from their canteen, they began making up packages of candy for the boys and girls. George donned his Santa garb and for the next ten years delivered treats and presents to the children.

At about the same time the Prince Rupert helicopter crew (the one that flew the old "62" Sikorski helicopter) thought it was about time that Santa arrived on the last supply run before Christmas. Even visiting only the stations with children, the chopper was full of parcels, food and mail. The trip was so much fun that it has become a Christmas tradition in the northern region as well. Jim West, a jovial Prince Rupert sign painter who has an enormous bushy beard and a tummy that "needs less padding every year," plays the part of St. Nick. He often brings along Mrs. Claus and even Granny Claus when she can spare the time away from her Christmas baking.

Pen, the southern Santa, and his wife, Betty, have a special affinity with the lights of this coast. One day about twenty years ago, when they were the keepers at Pine Island, a gale began to blow. Soon Pen, Betty and their two small girls had no choice but to flee to the higher land in the central part of the island. Before morning most of the station had been washed away. The marvellous gardens that Pen had so laboriously built, the helicopter pad, two fuel tanks. . . all were decimated. In the cold grey February dawn, they could see that the Pine Island lightstation had been destroyed.

With all their work washed away, the Browns decided that it was time to "retire" to Victoria. And when a Santa was needed, who better to take on the task than Pen, who adores children and understands the rigours of the lights?

About a week before Christmas the ship is loaded for the December supply run and with those supplies are sacks of specially chosen and wrapped presents from Eatons in Victoria. The Christmas wish lists have been compiled over the preceding months from each family and then mailed with the appropriate fanfare to S. Claus.

Most often the helicopter flies the gifts and Santa ashore, but sometimes he has to brave the work boat, changing from his rain gear into his bright red suit down on the dock or on the somewhat slippery shore. "It can be sort of awkward," Pen remarks.

As Santa Claus, Pen is beloved up and down the coast, but for his trials at Pine he is respected by the keepers as one of them.

Mabel was the Browns' pet duck on Pine Island. If you don't have a ready supply of full-flavoured duck eggs, substitute five large hen's eggs, stiffly beating the whites of three of them.

½ cup	butter or margarine	125 mL
1 cup	granulated sugar	250 mL
4	duck eggs, separated	4
1 cup	all-purpose flour	250 mL
2 tsps	baking powder	10 mL
2 tsps	cornstarch	10 mL
⅛ tsp	salt	.5 mL
½ cup	milk	125 mL
½ tsp	vanilla	2 mL
½ tsp	lemon extract (optional)	2 mL

Preheat the oven to 350°F (180°C).

In a large mixing bowl, cream the butter and the sugar until fluffy. Beat in the egg yolks, one at a time. Sift or stir together the flour, baking powder, cornstarch and salt. Add alternately with the milk to the creamed mixture. Whip two of the egg whites until very stiff, reserving the other two for another use, and gently fold into the batter with the vanilla and lemon extract.

Grease and flour two 8″ (20 cm) cake pans. Divide the batter evenly between them and bake for 20 minutes or until a needle inserted into the centre of them comes out clean.

Fill with Lemon Cheese (p. 122) or frost with Orange Butter Icing (below).

Makes one 8″ (20 cm) layer cake.

Orange Butter Icing

⅓ cup	softened butter	75 mL
3 cups	icing sugar	750 mL
¼ cup	milk or cream	50 mL
2 tsps	grated orange or lemon rind	10 ml

Cream the butter and icing sugar. Whip in the milk until the icing is fluffy. Stir in the orange rind.

Makes enough icing for one 8″ (20 cm) layer cake.

Strawberry Birthday Cake

Janet, Jerry, Jake and Justine Etzkorn   *Carmanah Point*

Packed carefully among the provisions aboard the *George R. Pearkes* were the fresh strawberries that would add the finishing touch to this special cake for Justine's third birthday. Carmanah Point is close enough to Victoria that the berries arrived in perfect condition.

Janet suggests assembling this cake a day early to allow it to set before serving. The sponge cake may be baked several days in advance and frozen or stored in a tightly covered container.

Sponge Cake

5	eggs	5
2 cups	granulated sugar	500 mL
2½ cups	all-purpose flour	625 mL
1 tsp	baking powder	5 mL
¼ cup	butter	50 mL
1 cup	milk	250 mL
1 tsp	vanilla	5 mL
1 tsp	lemon extract	5 mL

Preheat the oven to 325°F (160°C).

In a large bowl, beat the eggs until they are quite frothy and lemony in colour. Still beating, add the sugar slowly. Stir the flour and baking powder together. Add it, a little at a time, to the egg/sugar mixture, beating well after each addition.

Heat the butter and the milk to boiling in a small saucepan. Pour over the flour mixture and mix thoroughly. Stir in the vanilla and lemon extract. Pour into an ungreased 10″ (3 L) tube pan. Bake for 45–55 minutes, or until a testing needle comes out clean. Cool in the pan before cutting into 1″ (2.5 cm) cubes.

Strawberry Mixture

1 cup	boiling water	250 mL
2 3 oz.	packages strawberry gelatin	285 g
2 15 oz.	packages frozen strawberries, slightly thawed	2 435 g
2 cups	heavy cream (35%)	500 mL
	fresh strawberries, as needed	

In a large bowl, dissolve the gelatin in the boiling water. Add the strawberries and stir until the mixture begins to thicken. Whip 1 cup (250 mL) of the cream and fold it into the strawberry mixture. Gently fold in the cubes of sponge cake. Scrape the mixture into a large, deep bowl. Cover with plastic wrap and chill overnight.

Just before serving, turn it out onto a large platter. Whip the remaining cream and spread it all over the cake. If your supply ship arrives, garnish with whole fresh strawberries.

Makes 12 servings.

Lise's Carrot Nut Cake with Almond Cream Cheese Frosting

Lise, Ken and Noah Brunn   *Langara Point*

Geologists have visited Langara on and off for many years, pulling together all the fragments that they can to study the history of the Charlottes. It appears that 120 million years ago a massive tectonic change began. The Farallon Plate began to slide beneath the continent and is still moving and shaking. There are more quakes in the Charlottes than anywhere else in Canada. Only a few kilometres off the shore, the depth abruptly drops to thousands of fathoms where the plate begins.

The geologists have left behind all sorts of core samples and cuttings which little Noah has collected systematically. On the day that I was their guest we had great fun examining the contents of his jars and tins which were unceremoniously dumped all over the kitchen table.

1 cup	all-purpose flour	250 mL
1 cup	cake flour	250 mL
2 tsps	baking powder	10 mL
1 tsp	baking soda	5 mL
1 tsp	salt	5 mL
2 tsps	cinnamon	10 mL
½ tsp	freshly grated nutmeg	2 mL
1 cup	vegetable or corn oil	250 mL
4	eggs	4
1 cup	granulated sugar	250 mL
1 cup	brown sugar, lightly packed	250 mL
3 cups	finely grated carrot	750 mL
1 cup	chopped walnuts	250 mL
1 cup	raisins	250 mL

Preheat the oven to 325°F (160°C).

Sift together the flours, baking powder, baking soda, salt, cinnamon and nutmeg. Set aside. In a large mixing bowl beat the oil and add the eggs, one at a time. Still beating, measure in the granulated and brown sugar. Mix in the sifted dry ingredients until well combined. Fold in the grated carrot, nuts and raisins, mixing well. Bake in a well-greased 10″ (25 cm) tube pan or a 9″ x 13″ (3.5 L) rectangular cake pan for about 1½ hours or until a needle inserted into the cake comes out clean.

Allow the cake to cool before frosting.

Makes one 10″ (25 cm) tube cake or one 9″ x 13″ (3.5 L) cake.

Almond Cream Cheese Frosting

2 oz	plain cream cheese, softened	57 g
1	egg yolk	1
⅓ cup	butter, at room temperature	75 mL
5	drops almond extract	5
2 cups	icing sugar	500 mL

Blend the cream cheese, egg yolk, butter and almond extract thoroughly. Beat in the icing sugar until light and fluffy. Spread over the cooled cake.

Makes about 1½ cups (375 mL) icing or enough to thinly frost Lise's Carrot Nut Cake.

Pineapple Carrot Bundt Cake

Cate Weir and Ian Crocker, Matthew and Peter   *Pachena Point*

The oldest original French lens on the BC coast still shines at Pachena. Strategically located on the West Coast Hiking Trail, it provides a welcome stopping-off point for at least 3000 hikers every year. But the climax came on the evening of May 28, 1985 when a cougar attacked a young boy near the Darling River, only two miles from the station. As Cate says, "If the lightkeepers hadn't been here, the child would have died." Fortunately when the boy's aunt arrived breathless at Pachena Lightstation, the keepers were able to alert Tofino Coast Guard Radio and the convergence of aid began. The H.M.C.S. *MacKenzie* came in from the sea and a big Labrador helicopter flew over from Comox Air Force Base. Within three hours the young victim was hospitalized in Victoria, where doctors administered 187 stitches. With no emergency centres on the trail, the lightkeepers and their families provide far more than aids to navigation.

3 cups	all-purpose flour	750 mL
1½ cups	granulated sugar	375 mL
2 tsps	cinnamon	10 mL
1½ tsps	baking soda	7 mL
1 tsp	salt	5 mL

1 tsp	baking powder	5 mL
1 cup	crushed pineapple, undrained	250 mL
3	eggs, beaten	3
1½ cups	vegetable oil	375 mL
2 tsps	vanilla	10 mL
1½ cups	chopped walnuts or pecans	375 mL
2 cups	grated raw carrot	500 mL

Glaze (optional)

½ cup	icing sugar	125 mL
¼ cup	finely grated raw carrot	50 mL
2 tsps	lemon juice	10 mL

Preheat the oven to 325°F (160°C).

Sift or stir together the flour, sugar, cinnamon, baking soda, salt and baking powder. Drain the pineapple, reserving the juice. Whisk together the eggs, oil, vanilla and reserved juice. Make a well in the centre of the dry ingredients and pour in the liquid. Beat well for 3 minutes. Fold in the pineapple, nuts and grated carrot. Spread the batter evenly in a greased and floured bundt pan. Bake for 1–1½ hours, or until testing needle comes out clean. If you wish to glaze the cake, combine the icing sugar, grated carrot and lemon juice. Drizzle over the warm cake. Cool before serving.

Makes 12–14 servings.

Pauline's Zucchini Cake

Pauline, Joe and Cindy Balmer   *Estevan Point*

This is a very moist cake that travels well...it doesn't even need icing.

1 cup	raisins	250 mL
¼ cup	water	50 mL
½ cup	softened shortening	125 mL
2 cups	granulated sugar	500 mL
2	eggs	2
1 tsp	vanilla	5 mL
3¾ cups	grated, peeled, raw zucchini	925 mL
1	apple, peeled, cored and grated	1
1 tsp	grated orange rind	5 mL
2 cups	all-purpose flour	500 mL
2 tsps	baking soda	10 mL
1 tsp	cinnamon	5 mL
½ tsp	salt	2 mL
1 cup	chopped nuts (optional)	250 mL

Preheat the oven to 350°F (180°C).

In a saucepan bring the raisins and the water to a boil. Remove from the heat and cool. Cream the shortening and sugar. Beat in the eggs, one at a time, until fluffy. Stir in the vanilla, zucchini, apple, orange rind, and cooled raisin mixture. Sift or stir together the flour, baking soda, cinnamon and salt. Combine with the creamed mixture, stirring until no dry spots remain. Fold in the nuts. Spread the batter evenly in a well-greased 9" x 13" (3.5 L) cake pan. Bake for 1 hour or until a testing needle comes out clean when inserted into the centre of the cake. Dust with icing sugar when cooled or serve plain, perhaps with a little ice cream.

Makes one 9" x 13" (3.5L) cake.

Mystery Cake

Judy and Stan Westhaver   *Egg Island*

Try this recipe, but for heaven's sake, don't tell anyone what they are eating — green tomatoes. The cake is moist and intriguing simply dusted with icing sugar or glazed with a thin frosting.

¾ cup	softened butter or margarine	175 mL
2 cups	granulated sugar	500 mL
3	eggs	3
2 tsps	vanilla	10 mL
2½ cups	all-purpose flour	625 mL
½ cup	cocoa	125 mL
2½ tsps	baking powder	12 mL
1 tsp	salt	5 mL
½ cup	milk	125 mL
2 tsps	grated orange rind	10 mL
2 cups	grated green tomato	500mL
1 cup	chopped walnuts or pecans	250 ml

Preheat the oven to 350°F (180°C).

Cream the butter, sugar, eggs and vanilla until light and fluffy. With a fork, combine the flour, cocoa, baking powder and salt in a separate bowl. Add the dry ingredients to the creamed mixture alternately with the milk. Fold in the orange rind, green tomato and nuts. Spread the batter evenly in a well-greased and floured 10" (25 cm) tube pan. Bake for 1 hour or until a needle inserted into the cake comes out free of batter. Cool for 5 minutes before removing from the pan.

Makes one 10" (25 cm) cake.

Date/Chocolate Chip Cake

Judy and Stan Westhaver   *Egg Island*

Ever since I was a little girl (was I ever little?) chocolate cake with date filling has been my ultimate favourite. This is an easier version than the one my mom used to make, but it still combines those two great ingredients, chocolate and dates. Aah—comfort foods!

1½ cups	boiling water	375 mL
1 cup	chopped dates	250 mL
1 tsp	baking soda	5 mL
½ cup	shortening	125 mL
½ tsp	salt	2 mL
1 cup	granulated sugar	250 ml
2	eggs	2
1½ cups	all-purpose flour	375 mL
¾ tsp	baking soda	4 mL
	or	
1 tsp	baking powder	5 mL

Topping

1 6 oz pkg	semi-sweet chocolate chips	1 170 g pkg
½ cup	brown sugar, lightly packed	125 mL
½ cup	chopped walnuts	125 mL

Pour the boiling water over the dates and 1 tsp (5 mL) of the baking soda; allow them to stand until cool.

Preheat the oven to 350°F (180°C).

In a medium-sized mixing bowl, cream the shortening, salt and sugar. Beat in the eggs, one at a time, until the mixture is light and fluffy. Pour in the date mixture, stirring to combine thoroughly.

With a fork, stir the flour with the baking soda or powder. Stir into the date mixture and when well combined pour the batter into a greased 7" x 11" (2 L) cake pan.

Combine the chocolate chips, brown sugar and nuts and sprinkle evenly over the batter. Bake for 40–45 minutes.

Makes about 10–12 servings.

Birthday Spice Cake

Etta, Matt, Steven and Bruce Martinelli *Quatsino*

Self reliance is the name of the game for most lightkeepers. The Martinellis are excellent examples of that in almost every way. Before coming to the lights, Matt taught English at Oregon State University. He now teaches his own two teenage sons, without the aid of the usual course of study provided by the British Columbia government. The boys are growing up confident in their own Renaissance-like environment in which they have learned everything from the traditional 3 R's to excellence in wood-carving. They make furniture from the timber that grows on the island and even carve model ships. As part of a tightly knit family, the boys are outgoing and well spoken, quite able to face life in any part of the world.

¾ cup	milk	175 ml
¼ cup	white vinegar	50 mL
⅔ cup	butter, at room temperature	150 mL
1 cup	brown sugar	250 mL
2	eggs	2
3	egg whites from the following frosting recipe	3
3 cups	all-purpose flour	750 mL
1 tbsp	baking powder	15 mL
⅛ tsp	salt	.5 mL
1 tsp	cinnamon	5 mL
¼ tsp	ground cloves	1 mL
½ tsp	allspice	2 mL
½ tsp	freshly grated nutmeg	2 mL
1 cup	boiling water	250 mL
2 tsps	baking soda	10 mL
½ cup	raisins (optional)	125 mL
½ cup	chopped walnuts (optional)	125 mL
	Coconut Frosting (see below)	

Preheat the oven to 350°F (180°C).

Combine the milk and vinegar. Set it aside to curdle. In a large mixing bowl, cream the butter and brown sugar. Add the 2 egg yolks. In a separate bowl, beat the 5 egg whites to soft peaks to add later. Sift together the flour, baking powder, salt, cinnamon, cloves, allspice and nutmeg. Beat into the creamed mixture alternately with the soured milk. Fold in the egg whites gently. Combine the boiling water and baking soda and stir into the batter. Fold in the raisins or currants, and the nuts. Pour evenly into a well-greased

9″ x 13″ (3.5 L) cake pan. Bake for 25–35 minutes or until a testing needle comes out clean. Cool before frosting.

Coconut Frosting

1 cup	evaporated milk	250 mL
½ cup	granulated or brown sugar	125 mL
3	egg yolks	3
½ cup	butter	125 mL
1 tsp	brandy or vanilla	5 mL
1½–2 cups	shredded coconut	375–500 mL
1 cup	chopped walnuts, almonds or pecans	250 mL

Combine the milk, sugar, egg yolks, butter and brandy or vanilla in a heavy saucepan. Cook gently over medium-low heat until the mixture thickens. Stir in the coconut and the nuts. Beat with a wooden spoon until the frosting is cool and thick enough to spread.

Makes enough to top one 9″ x 13″ (3.5 L) cake.

Very Light Sponge Cake

Frances Collette   *Merry Island*

The Collettes have just retired from lightkeeping but when I met them, they were the sole proprietors of this pretty station just off the Sechelt Peninsula, a little piece of rock liberally covered with wild nodding onions and nose-tickling yarrow.

Serve this feathery cake with fresh berries and whipped cream or just mix a little orange juice and icing sugar to drizzle over it.

9	eggs, separated	9
½ tsp	salt	2 mL
¾ tsp	cream of tartar	4 mL
1¼ cups	granulated sugar	300 mL
2 tsps	grated lemon rind	10 mL
2 tbsps	fresh lemon juice	25 mL
2½ tbsps	water	30 mL
1¼ cups	sifted cake flour	300 mL

Preheat the oven to 350°F (180°C).

Combine the egg whites and the salt in a large mixing bowl. Beat until foamy. Add the cream of tartar and continue beating until shiny peaks are formed. Gradually add ½ cup (125 mL) of the sugar, sprinkling 2 tbsps (25 mL) at a time over the beaten egg whites, and whipping well after each addition. Continue beating until a stiff meringue is formed.

In a separate bowl beat the egg yolks until thick and lemon-coloured. Gradually pour in the remaining ¾ cup (175 mL) sugar, blending thoroughly. Combine the rind, lemon juice and water. Add to the yolk mixture. Still beating, mix in the flour. Fold the yolk mixture into the meringue gently until no dry spots remain. Pour into an ungreased 10" (25 cm) tube pan, spreading evenly. Bake for 45–50 minutes or until the top of the cake is golden and dry looking. Invert to cool. Loosen the edges before removing from the pan.

Makes one 10" (25 cm) cake.

Everyday Light Fruit Cake

Kay and Fred Pratt   *Ballenas Island*

The jet fighter had the junior keeper's house in its sights and was making ready to neutralize us all until it veered off into the cloudless sky. The Ballenas Island light is a directional finder and any poor tourist like myself loses a few years upon finding herself gently conversing about food in the living room, as a military aircraft begins its hourly game of chicken with the lightstation.

This fruit cake is so easy to make that it really is an everyday version, one that need not be baked just at Christmas.

¾ cup	raisins	175 mL
¾ cup	whole glazed cherries	175 mL
1	glazed pineapple ring, diced	1
1¾ cups	all-purpose flour	425 mL
1 cup	butter, softened	250 mL
¾ cup	granulated sugar	175 mL
2	eggs, beaten	2
¼ cup	milk	50 mL
2 tbsps	rum	25 mL
	or	
1 tsp	vanilla	5 mL
1 tsp	baking powder	5 mL
½ tsp	salt	2 mL

Preheat the oven to 325°F (160°C).

Grease an 8½" x 4½" x 3" (1.5 L) loaf pan and either flour it or line it with waxed paper.

In a small bowl, toss together the raisins, cherries, pineapple and ¼ cup (50 mL) of the flour.

Whip the butter and sugar together in a medium-sized bowl. Add the eggs, one at a time, creaming thoroughly after each. Still beating, pour in the milk and rum or vanilla.

Stir together the remaining flour, baking powder and salt. Gradually combine the dry ingredients with creamed mixture. Fold in the floured fruit and scrape the batter into the prepared loaf pan.

Bake for 1¼ hours or until a testing needle comes out clean. Turn out onto a rack and let cool completely before removing the waxed paper. Wrap in plastic for storage.

Makes one 8½" x 4½" x 3" (1.5 L) loaf.

Brazil Nut Christmas Cake

Dan Earl   *Sisters Island*

A few years ago Dan's doctor told him to quit his job at the University of British Columbia or else! So Dan became a free spirit, lightkeeping for two-week stints and building his boat, the *Dame Gracie*, on Thetis Island, one of the magnificent little gems that dot the Georgia Strait. He took up wood-carving and became a top-notch cook, probably out of necessity...most men who "batch it" on the lights live out of tins and boxes.

Try this for a special Christmas cake and don't forget to tell everyone whose recipe it is. Somehow the fact that it comes from a lonely wind-whipped lightstation makes it a little more special.

¾ cup	all-purpose flour	175 mL
½ tsp	baking powder	2 mL
½ tsp	salt	2 mL
3	eggs	3
¾ cup	fireweed honey or any other unpasteurized wildflower honey	175 mL
1 tsp	vanilla	5 mL
3 cups	shelled, whole Brazil nuts	750 mL
1 lb	whole pitted dates	450 g
1 cup	whole glazed cherries (red and green)	250 mL
6	candied pineapple rings (red, green and yellow), cut into quarters	6

Preheat the oven to 300°F (150°C).

Line a 9″ x 5″ x 2½″ (2 L) loaf pan with heavy brown paper and grease generously.

In a small bowl, stir together the flour, baking powder and salt. Beat the eggs, honey and vanilla together in a large mixing bowl. Add the dry ingredients, combining thoroughly. Fold in the nuts, dates, cherries and pineapple. Scrape the batter into the prepared loaf pan. Place a pan of hot water on the lowest rack of the oven. Bake the fruit cake for 1¾–2 hours or until a testing needle comes out clean.

Makes one 9″ x 5″ x 2½″ (2 L) loaf.

Chocolate Chip Banana Cupcakes

Judy and Stan Westhaver   *Egg Island*

Although these cupcakes are excellent served plain, a little dollop of whipped cream and some fresh berries are nice on the side.

½ cup	softened shortening	125 mL
1 cup	granulated sugar	250 mL
2	eggs	2
1 tsp	vanilla	5 mL
1 cup	mashed ripe banana	250 mL
2¼ cups	cake flour	300 mL
½ tsp	salt	2 mL
2½ tsps	baking powder	12 mL
½ tsp	baking soda	2 mL
¼ cup	buttermilk or sour milk	50 mL
1	6 oz (170 g) package semi-sweet chocolate chips	1

Preheat the oven to 375°F (190°C).

In a large mixing bowl, cream the shortening and sugar. Beat in the eggs, vanilla and banana and mix thoroughly. Sift the flour, salt, baking powder and baking soda together. Gently fold into the creamed mixture alternately with the milk. Stir in the chocolate chips. Spoon the batter into paper-lined muffin tins. Bake for 20–25 minutes.

Makes 18 large cupcakes.

Flaky Pastries: from Apple Pie to Butter Tarts

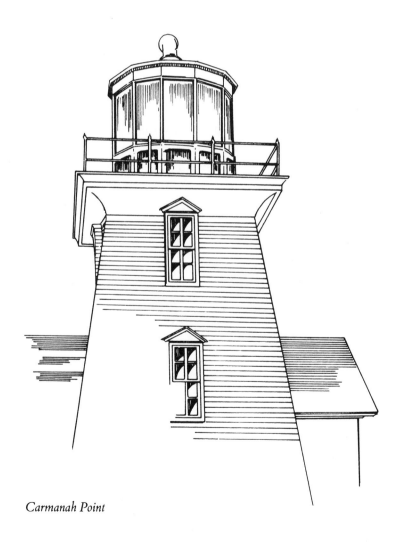

Carmanah Point

Mom's Basic Pastry

Pauline, Joe and Cindy Balmer   *Estevan Point*

It just may be that, contrary to popular belief, Estevan Point, and the adjacent Indian village of Hesquiat, was the location of the first contact between white men and natives on the west coast of Canada. The log book of the Spanish ship *Santiago* noted that in June of 1774 contact was made with the Hesquiat band. It was later confirmed by Father Brabant, one of the early priests who attempted to preserve the the oral history of the coastal Indians, that indeed the Hesquiats had seen what they thought were their dead ones returning in an oarless canoe. The passengers of the ship were not spectres from the past, but rather odd looking men who wanted to trade.

The village of Hesquiat now has one rather ramshackle house surrounded by junk and entangled in wild blackberry vines and weeds. It is a sad but not unique conclusion to a noble story.

Pauline swears by this recipe, which is her mother's. It is almost fool-proof.

5½ cups	all-purpose flour	1.375 L
1 tsp	brown sugar	5 mL
1 tsp	baking powder	5 mL
½ tsp	salt	2 mL
1 lb	lard or vegetable shortening, chilled	450 g
1	egg, lightly beaten	1
1 tbsp	vinegar or lemon juice	15 mL
¾–1 cup	ice water	175–250 mL

In a large mixing bowl, stir together the flour, brown sugar, baking powder and salt. Cut in the lard or shortening until the mixture resembles fine crumbs. In a separate bowl, whisk together the egg, vinegar and ice water. Make a well in the dry ingredients and pour in the liquid, stirring gently with a fork to combine. The dough will form a ball. Turn it out onto a floured board and knead 2 or 3 times before rolling with a well-floured rolling pin. After rolling, the pie shells may be tightly covered in plastic wrap and frozen until needed.

Makes enough pastry for two 9″ (23 cm) double crust pies plus 12 tart shells, or for five 9″ (23 cm) single crust pies.

Ivory Island

Almost Instant Pie Crust

Judy, Gorden and Guthrie Schweers   *Ivory Island*

This is without a doubt the fastest baked pie shell that I have ever made. I was very sceptical about how it would taste, but we were all very impressed. It's great filled with Wendy Abram's Homemade Chocolate Pudding (p. 144).

1½ cups	all-purpose flour	375 mL
2 tsps	granulated sugar	10 mL
1 tsp	salt	5 mL
½ cup	vegetable oil	125 mL
2 tbsps	milk	25 mL

Preheat the oven to 425°F (220°C).

Sift the flour, sugar and salt into a 9″ (22 cm) pie plate. Whisk the oil and milk with a fork until the mixture turns quite creamy and thick. Combine with the flour mixture until it is crumbly and no dry spots remain. Pat it firmly into the shape of a crust. I used a flat-bottomed glass to finish the base. flute the edge carefully. Prick the surface and bake for 10–12 minutes or until golden. Remove from the oven and cool until needed.

Makes one 9″ (22 cm) pie shell.

Old-Fashioned Apple Pie

Judy and Stan Westhaver   *Egg Island*

As I am writing, one of these pies is baking its way into the memories of my kids...they love to come home from school to such incredible treats.

1	8″ (20 cm) unbaked pie shell	1
½ cup plus 2 tbsps	all-purpose flour	150 mL
½ cup	granulated sugar	125 mL
¼ tsp	cinnamon	1 mL
¼ tsp	freshly grated nutmeg	1 mL
4	large cooking apples, peeled, cored and thinly sliced	4
½ cup	brown sugar	125 mL
½ cup	chilled butter	125 mL
	sour cream as needed, for garnish	

Preheat the oven to 425°F (220°C).

Blend 2 tbsps (25 mL) of the flour with the granulated sugar and the spices. Toss with the sliced apples. Pile into the unbaked pastry crust. In a small bowl, stir the brown sugar with the remaining ½ cup (125 mL) flour. With a pastry blender or two knives, cut in the butter until it looks like coarse crumbs. Sprinkle evenly over the apples. Bake for 10 minutes. Reduce the heat to 350°F (180°C) and continue to bake for an additional 40 minutes or until the apples are tender. Serve with dollops of sour cream.

Makes 6 servings.

Dried Apple Pie

Judy and Stan Westhaver   *Egg Island*

Judy writes, "This is handy for people who live in isolated areas because it is something we can keep on our shelves all the time." But it's enough to make anyone keep dried apples, or "schnitz," as my Mennonite friends call them, in their cupboard.

1 cup	dried apples	250 mL
2½ cups	hot water	625 mL
¼ tsp	salt	1 mL
⅔ cup	granulated sugar	150 mL
⅛ tsp	cinnamon	.5 mL
1 tbsp	lemon juice	15 mL

4 tsps	cornstarch	20 mL
1/4 cup	cold water	50 mL
1	9" (22 cm) double crust pie shell, unbaked	1
1 tbsp	butter	15 mL

Preheat the oven to 425°F (220°C).

Place the apples, hot water and salt in a saucepan and bring to a boil over medium heat. Cover and reduce the heat. Simmer, stirring occasionally, for 10–15 minutes or until the apples are tender. Blend in the sugar, cinnamon and lemon juice and continue to cook. Mix the cornstarch and water together; add to the saucepan. Cook and stir until thickened. Pour into the prepared pie shell, dot with butter and top with the upper crust. Seal the edges by crimping and slash the top to allow the steam to escape. Bake for 35–40 minutes.

Makes 6–8 servings.

Sour Cream Raisin Walnut Pie

Judy and Stan Westhaver   *Egg Island*

This is Judy's favourite pie.

1	10" (25 cm) baked pie shell (p. 117)	1
1 cup	granulated sugar	250 mL
1 tbsp	cornstarch	15 mL
1/4 tsp	salt	1 mL
1 tsp	cinnamon	5 mL
1/2 tsp	freshly grated nutmeg	2 mL
1/4 tsp	ground cloves	1 mL
1 cup	sour cream	250 mL
1 tbsp	lemon juice	15 mL
1 cup	raisins	250 mL
2	eggs, separated	2
1/2 cup	walnuts	125 mL
1/4 tsp	cream of tartar	1 mL

Preheat the oven to 350°F (180°C).

In a heavy saucepan, combine ¾ cup (175 mL) of the sugar, the cornstarch, salt, cinnamon, nutmeg and cloves. Whisk in the sour cream and lemon juice. Add the raisins and bring to a boil over medium heat, stirring constantly until thickened. In a small bowl, beat the egg yolks. Whisk a little of the filling into the yolks, then return to the hot mixture. Cook gently, stirring, for 1 minute. Fold in the walnuts and pour into the baked pastry crust.

Beat the egg whites until stiff. Still beating, add the cream of tartar and the remaining ¼ cup (50 mL) sugar, a spoonful at a time. The meringue should be thick, stiff and glossy. Pile on top of the filling and bake for 8–10 minutes or until it begins to turn golden.

Makes 8–10 servings.

Judy makes a great no bake pie shell by combining equal parts of dates and desicated coconut. She says that 1 × cups (300mL) each will be enough for a 9″ (22cm) pie. Grind the two ingredients together and pat evenly into the pie plate. Great with a chiffon type filling. (Judy Schweers, Ivory Island)

Julia's Butter Tarts

Lise, Ken and Noah Brunn   *Langara Point*

Julia Moe is not only a good friend of the Brunns, she is an accomplished and published poet. While she was the keeper at Kains Island, she put together a collection of her works that reflect with insight and love her life on the lights.

Lise bakes these tarts in a broken oil stove that takes all day to heat up, but when it does, watch out!

Pastry

2 cups	all-purpose flour	500 ml
1 tsp	salt	5 mL
¾ cup	chilled lard	175 mL
	ice water, as needed	

Filling

½ cup	raisins	125 mL
	boiling water, as needed	
¼ cup	butter	50 mL
½ cup	brown sugar, lightly packed	125 mL
¼ tsp	salt	1 mL
½ cup	corn syrup	125 mL

1	egg, beaten	1
½ tsp	vanilla	2 mL
	a few drops lemon juice	

Preheat the oven to 375°F (190°C) or 300°F (150°C) if your stove is broken like Lise's.

Prepare the pastry. Stir together the flour and salt. Cut in the lard with a pastry blender, until it resembles coarse crumbs. With a fork, stir in enough ice water to hold the dough loosely together, about ⅓ cup (75 mL). Gather into a ball and chill for 10–15 minutes before rolling. Roll on a lightly floured surface until the pastry is about ¼″ (6 mm) thick. Line 12 tart tins with it.

Prepare the filling. Soak the raisins in boiling water to cover. Drain well when the edges of the raisins begin to turn white. Cream the butter and sugar and add the salt, corn syrup, egg, vanilla and lemon juice. Fold in the raisins. Spoon into the unbaked tart shells until they are about ⅔ full. Bake for 20–25 minutes.

Makes 1 dozen.

Raspberry Coconut Tarts

Pauline, Joe and Cindy Balmer   *Estevan Point*

Pauline sends her monthly food order to Woodwards in Victoria aboard the tender ship—in this case it was the *George R. Pearkes*—to be forwarded to her the following month. She keeps 24–30 quarts of milk in the freezer, plus meat, fish and any other perishables. Consequently, there is just no room for bread, pastries and cakes...they all are baked fresh every several days. She says that when the work crews arrive, feeding them is nothing short of "horrendous." There are up to eleven men, who work from sunrise to dusk and eat simply gargantuan meals. Add to that their own family of four and it means that Pauline and her daughter are cooking all day long. It reminds me of the tales my grandparents used to tell of the huge threshing dinners at harvest-time in Ontario...an absolute orgy of eating.

	unbaked pastry for 12 tart shells	
¼ cup	raspberry jam	50 mL
1	egg	1
⅛ tsp	salt	.5 mL
1 tsp	vanilla	5 mL
½ cup	shredded coconut	125 mL
¼ cup	chopped candied cherries	50 mL
¼ cup	melted butter	50 mL

Preheat the oven to 425°F (220°C).

Place 1 tsp (5 mL) jam into each unbaked tart shell. Beat the egg with the salt and vanilla. Stir in the coconut, candied cherries and melted butter. Spoon filling evenly into the tart shells. Bake for 10 minutes, then reduce the heat to 350°F (180°C) for an additional 5 minutes or until the filling is set.

Makes one dozen medium-sized tarts.

Lemon Cheese

Judy and Stan Westhaver   *Egg Island*

Stored in the refrigerator, Lemon Cheese or Lemon Curd, as it's known in other parts of the world, is a great help when people "drop in" (and on a lightstation, that's the literal meaning). fill baked tartlet shells or spread it in a jelly roll for a special dessert.

3	lemons	3
6	eggs	6
2 cups	granulated sugar	500 mL
½ cup	butter	125 mL

Grate the rind of 2 lemons. Squeeze the juice from all 3 lemons. Put the rind and the juice into the top of a double boiler. Whisk in the eggs and the sugar and place over simmering water. Cook, stirring frequently, until the mixture thickens, about 15–20 minutes. Add the butter and stir to combine. Remove from the heat and allow to cool slightly before using. Store in a glass container in the refrigerator. It will keep for several months.

Makes about 3 cups (750 mL).

Puffy Apple Turnovers

Linda and Don Weeden   *Cape Scott*

These buttery turnovers are wonderful, puffy and filled with fragrant apple. Vary the fruit fillings with the season and be sure to bake a double batch because they freeze well—if they make it that far. Mine didn't!

Puff Pastry

2 cups	all-purpose flour	500 mL
1 cup	chilled butter	250 mL
½ cup	ice water	125 mL

Filling

2	large cooking apples, peeled, cored and coarsely chopped (I suggest Northern Spies or Ida Reds)	2
1 tbsp	water	15 mL
1 tsp	lemon juice	5 mL
½ cup	granulated sugar	125 mL
1 tbsp	cornstarch	15 mL
¼ tsp	cinnamon	1 mL
¼ tsp	grated nutmeg (optional)	1 mL

Egg Wash

1	egg, beaten	1
1 tbsp	water	15 mL

Icing

½ cup	icing sugar	125 mL
½ tsp	vanilla	2 mL
2–3 tsps	water or milk	10–15 mL

To prepare the pastry, measure the flour into a small mixing bowl. With a pastry blender, cut in ½ cup (125 mL) of the butter until the mixture has the consistency of fine crumbs. Sprinkle with the water, mixing well with a fork. Gather up into a ball.

On a lightly floured surface roll the dough into a 8″ x 18″ (10 x 44 cm) rectangle. Slice ¼ cup (50 mL) of the butter thinly and lay evenly on ⅔ of the pastry. Fold into thirds and roll again into a rectangle 8″ x 18″ (10 x 44 cm). Repeat with the remaining butter, but before rolling, wrap in plastic and chill for 15 minutes. After chilling, re-roll into the same sized rectangle, fold lengthwise, then crosswise. Wrap in plastic and chill for 1 hour.

In a heavy saucepan, stir together the apples, water and lemon juice. Cover and steam on medium-low heat for 5–10 minutes or until the apples are almost tender. Stir together the sugar, cornstarch and spices. Add to the filling and continue to cook, uncovered, until thickened. Remove from the heat and chill until ready to use. Preheat the oven to 425°F (220°C).

Roll the dough into the now infamous rectangle (see above) and cut in half crosswise. Roll each half into a 12″ (30 cm) square. Cut each square into quarters. Brush lightly with the egg wash made by whisking the egg and water together. Spoon ⅛ of the filling onto the centre of each square. Fold diagonally and seal tightly. Place onto a baking sheet. Brush with a little more egg wash and slash the top several times to allow the steam to escape.

Bake for 20–25 minutes or until richly golden. Remove from the oven and cool on racks. Stir the icing sugar, vanilla and water together and when the turnovers are almost cool, swirl and drizzle this icing all over them.

Makes 8 large turnovers.

Old-Fashioned Squares and Cookies

Lennard Island

Fancy Chocolate Brownies

Janet, Jerry, Justine and Jake Etzkorn   *Carmanah Point*

The Easter Bunny doesn't leave eggs for Jake and Justine, the Etzkorn children. He, she or it hides the mysterious glass floats that wash in from Japan. Early each Easter morning, the family put on their rubber boots and head down to the shoreline to start the hunt. The kids have boxes full of these glassy treasures. All along the miles of beach that form the Pacific Rim National Park, the Kuro Shio, or Japanese current, has provided flotsam and jetsam in the form of the beautiful glass balls. Every now and then you'll find a piece of bamboo or a plastic container scribbled with Japanese. The current seems to be aimed almost directly from Japan to Vancouver Island before it sweeps up towards Alaska and down to California.

When I flew into Carmanah it was Justine's third birthday. Her grandma, Evelyn Etzkorn, was on board also, visiting from Canmore, Alberta and as anxious as anyone could be to see her family. Justine stood waving in her new red velvet party dress as the chopper landed. She took us to the house where Janet had just finished decorating a big plate of these yummy brownies complete with rosettes and candy sprinkles. What more could a little girl want?

Brownies

2 1 oz squares	unsweetened chocolate	2 28 g squares
½ cup	butter	125 mL
1 cup	granulated sugar	250 mL
2	eggs	2
1 tsp	vanilla	5 mL
¾ cup	all-purpose flour	175 mL
½ tsp	baking powder	2 mL
1 cup	finely chopped nuts	250 mL

Frosting

2 1 oz squares	unsweetened chocolate	2 28 g squares
⅓ cup	butter	75 mL
¾ cup	icing sugar	175 mL
2 tsps	cream or milk	10 mL
	candy cake decorations, as needed	

Preheat the oven to 350°F (180°C).

Melt 1 oz (28 g) of the chocolate and the butter in the top of a double boiler with simmering water below.

In a large bowl, beat together the sugar and the eggs until creamy and light. Whip in the chocolate mixture and the vanilla. Still beating, sift in the flour and baking powder. Fold in the nuts. Spread evenly in a lightly greased 8″ (2 L) square cake pan. Bake for 25 minutes or until a needle comes out clean when inserted into the centre. Cool before slicing into squares. Decorate just before serving.

To make the frosting, melt and cool 1 oz (28 g) of the chocolate over simmering water. Cream the butter, chocolate and icing sugar. Add the cream and continue to beat until fluffy. Janet uses a pastry bag with a star tip to pipe neat little rosettes on the top of each brownie. Then she sprinkles them with candy cake decorations, much to the delight of the children.

Makes 2–3 dozen brownies.

Apple-Oatmeal Wheat Bars

Linda and Don Weeden   *Cape Scott*

It's this kind of wonderful treat that welcomes visitors like the captain and crew of the *Thomas Crosby V*, the United Church's mission ship that regularly stops by the more remote stations. Over a cup of coffee, life's difficulties are hashed over, world events are discussed and the keepers are kept in touch with happenings other than the day-to-day monotony of doing weather reports and monitoring navigation. It's Christianity in action.

¼ cup	all-purpose flour	50 mL
¾ tsp	baking powder	4 mL
½ tsp	baking soda	2 mL
1 tsp	cinnamon	5 mL
½ tsp	freshly grated nutmeg	2 mL
½ tsp	salt	2 mL
½ cup	wholewheat flour	125 mL
⅓ cup	shortening	75 mL
¾ cup	brown sugar	175 mL
2	eggs, beaten	2
¼ cup	milk	50 mL
1 cup	oatmeal	250 mL
¼ cup	wheat germ	50 mL
3 cups	peeled, diced apples	750 mL
½ cup	chopped walnuts	125 ml
	icing sugar, as needed	
	or	
	a glaze made of ½ cup (125 mL) icing sugar and 2 tsps (10 mL) water	

Preheat the oven to 375°F (190°C).

Sift or stir together the flour, baking powder, baking soda, cinnamon, nutmeg and salt. Stir in the wholewheat flour. Set aside.

In a large mixing bowl, cream the shortening and brown sugar until light. Add the eggs, one at a time, and continue to beat. Blend in the milk, then the flour mixture. Stir in the oatmeal, wheat germ, apples and walnuts. Turn into a greased 9" x 13" (3.5 L) pan. Bake for 35–40 minutes. Let cool on a wire rack before dusting with icing sugar or drizzling with the glaze.

We like this dessert with whipped cream, lightly sweetened and dusted with cinnamon.

Makes 10–12 servings.

Cape Scott Squares

Linda and Don Weeden   *Cape Scott*

Much like the famous or infamous (depending on your hip size) Nanaimo bar.

Base

½ cup	corn syrup	125 mL
1 cup	peanut butter	250 mL
2 cups	crispy rice cereal	500 mL

Filling

¼ cup	softened butter	50 mL
2 tbsps	vanilla custard powder	25 mL
2 cups	icing sugar	500 mL
3 tbsps	milk	45 mL

Topping

3 tbsps	butter	45 mL
3 oz	semi-sweet chocolate	85 g

In a heavy-bottomed saucepan, gently heat the corn syrup with the peanut butter, stirring constantly to prevent sticking. Do not boil. Pour over the cereal in a well-buttered 9" x 13" (3.5 L) pan. Mix thoroughly and press it evenly onto the bottom of the pan to form a crust.

Cream the butter, custard powder and icing sugar, and add milk to thin it to the consistency of frosting. Spread it over the base.

Melt the butter and chocolate in a small bowl set in simmering water, or in the microwave on Medium for 2–3 minutes. Stir well and drizzle over the filling. Chill the squares completely before slicing.

Makes 3–4 dozen squares.

Coconut Dream Bars with Orange Frosting

Wendy, Jim, Jessie and Melissa Abram   *Cape Mudge*

When Wendy and Jim were keepers in the northern district, an engineer kept walking over a particular box, stowed "safely" in the ship's hold, before it was delivered to them with their other provisions. It turned out to be their monthly supply of 9 dozen eggs. The engineer is now known as "Crusher."

½ cup	softened butter	125 mL
1½ cups	brown sugar	325 mL
1 cup plus 2 tbsps	all-purpose flour	275 mL
½ tsp	salt	2 mL
1 tsp	baking powder	5 mL
1½ cups	shredded coconut	325 mL
1 cup	finely chopped nuts	250 mL
2	eggs	2
1 tsp	vanilla	5 mL

Orange Frosting

¼ cup	softened butter	50 mL
2 cups	icing sugar	500 mL
1 tsp	vanilla	5 mL
2 tbsps	orange juice concentrate, thawed	25 mL

Preheat the oven to 375°F (190°C).

Cream the butter and ½ cup (125 mL) of the brown sugar in a small mixing bowl. Add 1 cup (250 mL) of the flour and blend until the mixture is quite crumbly. Press into an 8" x 12" (3 L) baking pan. Bake for 10 minutes and allow to cool while you prepare the filling.

Stir the remaining 2 tbsps (25 mL) flour with the salt and the baking powder. Sprinkle over the coconut and nuts. Whisk together the eggs, remaining brown sugar and vanilla and combine it with the coconut mixture.

Bake for 20 minutes or until golden. Remove from the oven and cool slightly before icing and slicing into bars.

To make the frosting, cream the butter and icing sugar. Beat in the vanilla and enough of the orange juice concentrate to make a stiff icing. If more liquid is needed add a few drops of milk or water.

Makes 4–5 dozen bars.

Linda's Matrimonial Cake

Linda and Don Weeden   *Cape Scott*

This is a particularly delicious version of the classic date square recipe.

2 cups	chopped dates	500 mL
1 cup	water	250 mL
1½ cups	wholewheat flour	375 mL
1 tsp	baking powder	5 mL
½ tsp	baking soda	2 mL
1 cup	softened butter	250 mL
1 cup	brown sugar	250 mL
1½ cups	oatmeal	375 mL

To make the filling, cook the dates and water together in a heavy saucepan until the mixture is softened and smooth. Cool while making the crust.

Preheat the oven to 350°F (180°C).

In a large mixing bowl, blend the flour, baking powder and baking soda. With a fork, cut in the butter. Add the brown sugar and oatmeal, stirring until thoroughly mixed. Press half of this mixture into a 9″ x 9″ (2 L) square pan. Spread the filling evenly over it. Top with the remaining oatmeal crust, pressing lightly to smooth it. Bake for 20–25 minutes or until golden. Allow to cool in the pan before cutting into squares.

Makes about 3 dozen 1½″ (4 cm) squares.

Honey Granola Cookies

Darlene and Allan Tansky   *Scarlett Point*

The breakers were pounding unceasingly on the shore, but in the gut (small inlet) the work boat was busy slinging up lumber, groceries, craft supplies, a fragile package of forget-me-nots for Darlene to press into jewelery and of course, the long-awaited mail. From time to time, the noise from the logging camp on the other side of the island drifted over to the station.

Suddenly a chopper swirled down over the kelp-streaked, cerulean blue waters and touched down on the pad that has been the thorn in the side of the coast guard for several years: no matter how much money is spent, it just keeps on cracking. But it is the lifeline, and no matter the cost, it must be maintained.

1 cup	butter or margarine	250 mL
½ cup	brown sugar, packed	125 mL
½ cup	liquid honey	125 mL
2	eggs	2

½ cup	plain yogurt	125 mL
1 tsp	vanilla	5 mL
1½ cups	all-purpose flour	375 ml
1 tsp	baking soda	5 mL
1¾ cups	granola	425 mL
½ cup	semi-sweet chocolate chips	125 mL

Preheat the oven to 350°F (180°C).

Cream the butter, sugar, honey, eggs, yogurt and vanilla until light and fluffy. Stir the flour and baking soda together, and add it to the creamed mixture. Combine thoroughly. Fold in the granola and chocolate chips. Drop by teaspoonfuls onto a well-greased baking sheet. They should be at least 2″ (5 cm) apart because they spread considerably. Bake for 8–10 minutes or until golden.

Makes 5–6 dozen.

Christmasy Scotch Shortbread Diamonds

Lise, Ken and Noah Brunn   *Langara Point*

Langara is certainly one of the most demanding stations on the coast, but it is the most wildly beautiful in the northern district. The peregrine falcons and bald eagles nest here. The whales spout and the bouldered beach is home to sea otters and seals. Overhead the clouds scud by, chased by the gales of the Pacific. The weather is entirely unpredictable.

1 cup	butter, at room temperature	250 mL
½ cup	granulated sugar	125 mL
2½ cups	all-purpose flour	625 mL

Preheat the oven to 300°F (150°C).

Cream the butter and sugar until light. Stir in the flour. The dough will be crumbly at first, but work in the flour by hand until it becomes pliable. Chill several hours. Return to room temperature. Roll small chunks of dough on a lightly floured surface to ¼–½″ (6 mm–1 cm) thickness. Cut into diamond shapes and arrange on an ungreased baking sheet. Prick the surface of each cookie several times with a fork. Bake for about 20 minutes or until the diamonds are golden brown around the edges.

Makes about 3½ dozen.

Melt in Your Mouth Chocolate Chip Cookies!

Dan and Fil McMurray   *Pointer Island (now automated)*

Rice flour may be purchased from almost any supermarket. But if you have the facilities, you could grind long grain brown rice into flour, like Dan and Fil do. The results are really worth the effort.

2 cups	butter, softened	500 mL
2 cups	granulated sugar	500 mL
1 cup	brown sugar	250 mL
4	eggs	4
2 tsps	salt (optional)	10 mL
2 tsps	baking powder	10 mL
3 cups	all-purpose flour	750 mL
3 cups	rice flour	750 mL
1 12 oz pkg	semi-sweet chocolate chips	1 340 g pkg
4 tsps	vanilla	20 mL
½ cup	walnuts (optional)	125 mL

Preheat the oven to 350°F (180°C).

Cream the butter in a large mixing bowl. Beat in the sugars and add the eggs, one at a time, until fluffy and lemon-coloured.

In a separate bowl, stir together the salt, baking powder and flours. Add to the creamed mixture, blending thoroughly. Stir in the chocolate chips, vanilla and walnuts. Drop by teaspoonfuls onto lightly greased cookie sheets. Bake for 10–15 minutes.

Makes 11–12 dozen cookies.

Oatmeal Crunchies

Linda and Don Weeden   *Cape Scott*

If I were stranded on an island or perhaps if I were a lightkeeper and there was one oatmeal cookie recipe that I could keep, this is it.

½ cup	softened shortening	125 mL
½ cup	brown sugar	125 mL
1	egg, beaten	1
¼ tsp	vanilla	1 mL
½ cup	granulated sugar	125 mL
1 cup	all-purpose flour	250 mL
½ tsp	baking powder	2 mL
½ tsp	baking soda	2 mL
½ tsp	salt	2 mL

¾ cup	oatmeal	175 mL
¼ cup	chopped walnuts	50 mL
	extra granulated sugar, as needed	

Preheat the oven to 375°F (190°C).

Cream the shortening and brown sugar. Beat in the egg and vanilla until light and fluffy. Still beating, sift in the granulated sugar, flour, baking powder, baking soda and salt. Stir in the oatmeal and walnuts.

Shape the dough into small balls and dip the tops in granulated sugar. Place on well-greased cookie sheets and press down lightly with a fork. Bake for 10–12 minutes.

Makes 3–4 dozen crunchies.

Oatmeal Chocolate Chip Cookies

Judy and Stan Westhaver   *Egg Island*

The possibilities are endless with a basic recipe like this one. Replace the chocolate chips with raisins or currants; substitute wheat germ for part of the oatmeal; toss in coconut, chopped pecans or almonds to replace the walnuts...your imagination is the limit.

1 cup	shortening	250 mL
¾ cup	brown sugar, firmly packed	175 mL
¼ cup	granulated sugar	50 mL
1 tsp	vanilla	5 mL
1½ cups	all-purpose flour	375 mL
½ tsp	salt	2 mL
1 tsp	baking soda	5 mL
¼ cup	boiling water	50 mL
2 cups	quick-cooking oatmeal	500 mL
½ cup	chopped walnuts	125 ml
1 6 oz pkg	semi-sweet chocolate chips	1 170 g pkg

Preheat the oven to 350°F (180°C).

In a large mixing bowl, cream the shortening, sugars and vanilla until light and fluffy. Stir in the flour and salt. Dissolve the baking soda in the boiling water and add it to the creamed mixture. Stir in the oatmeal, walnuts and chocolate chips, mixing until well blended.

Drop the batter by heaping teaspoonfuls onto greased baking sheets about 2" (5 cm) apart. Bake for 10–12 minutes.

Makes about 6 dozen cookies.

Oatmeal Cookies

Margaret and Tony Holland   *Lennard Island*

Once the waves were so high that a young seaman missed his footing while climbing down into the work boat and fell, spread-eagled, into the ocean. It was at that point that I decided not to attempt to visit Lennard. Even if I wore a survival suit, it would be a chilling experience, and the landing at the island is on surf-torn rock.

2 cups	quick-cooking oatmeal	500mL
¾ cup	all-purpose flour	175 mL
½ cup	granulated sugar	125 mL
1 tsp	baking soda	5 mL
½ cup	butter or margarine	125 mL
¼ cup	golden syrup	50 mL
1 tbsp	cold water	15 mL

Preheat the oven to 375°F (190°C).

Stir together the oatmeal, flour, sugar and soda. In a small saucepan, heat the butter and syrup slowly until it begins to bubble. Stir into the dry ingredients, adding the water to make the dough workable. Form into small balls and place on a greased baking sheet. Press down lightly with a fork dipped in water. Bake for 7–8 minutes.

Makes 3–4 dozen.

Sesame Seed Cookies

Linda and Don Weeden   *Cape Scott*

Built in 1959 to help guide the Alcan Aluminum ships to their new smelter at Kitimat, Cape Scott is perched at the northernmost tip of Vancouver Island. I visited the light with Herb Buchanan, the former Director General of west coast operations for the Canadian Coast Guard and his wife, Kay. We decided that we must walk to the foghorns on the tip of the station property. No one told us it would be a mile on boardwalks that sometimes swing over deep gorges, or that it was mostly uphill. By the time we puffed up the final ridge, the wind blowing directly off the Pacific had begun to buffet us. We looked out towards Triangle Island, the location of an ill-fated lightstation where, nearly eighty years ago, the keeper's cow had been blown off the edge into the boiling sea and the men were reduced to crawling on their bellies from one shaking building to the next. As we stood on the foghorn's platform, our clothes flapping wildly in the wind, we began to understand the forces with which the keepers of the lights have to contend.

2½ cups	all-purpose flour	625 mL
1 tsp	baking soda	5 mL
1 tsp	salt	5 mL
1 tsp	cinnamon	5 mL
1 cup	vegetable oil	250 mL
2 cups	brown sugar	500 mL
2	eggs, beaten	2
⅓ cup	milk	75 mL
2½ cups	oatmeal	625 mL
1½ cups	sesame seeds	375 mL
1 cup	raisins	250 mL

Preheat the oven to 350°F (180°C).

Sift the flour, baking soda, salt and cinnamon together. Set aside. Using an electric mixer, beat together the oil and sugar in a large mixing bowl. Add the eggs and milk, beating thoroughly to combine. Stir in the oatmeal, sesame seeds and the flour mixture. Toss in the raisins and mix well. Drop by spoonfuls onto well-greased cookie sheets. Bake for 8–10 minutes or until beginning to turn golden.

Makes 8 dozen small cookies, perfect for the lunchbox set.

Sour Cream Chocolate Chip Cookies with Maple-Butter Glaze

Gwen and Doug Fraser   *Pine Island*

These soft, chewy cookies are even better with the buttery glaze.

½ cup	shortening	125 mL
1½ cups	brown sugar, packed	375 mL
1 cup	sour cream	250 mL
1 tsp	vanilla	5 mL
2¾ cups	all-purpose flour	675 mL
1 tsp	salt	5 mL
½ tsp	baking soda	2 mL
1 cup	semi-sweet chocolate chips	250 mL

Maple Butter Glaze

½ cup	butter or margarine	125 mL
2 cups	icing sugar	500 mL
1–2 tsps	maple flavouring	5–10 mL
3 tbsps	hot water	45 mL

Preheat the oven to 375°F (190°C).

Cream the shortening and brown sugar. Add the sour cream and vanilla, beating until fluffy. Stir together the flour, salt and baking soda. Combine the dry ingredients with the creamed mixture. Fold in the chocolate chips. Drop dough by level tablespoonfuls about 2" (5 cm) apart onto ungreased cookie sheets. Bake for 10 minutes and immediately remove the cookies from the sheets to cool.

Prepare the glaze by heating the butter over low heat until golden brown. Remove from the heat. Stir in the icing sugar and maple flavouring to taste. Beat in enough hot water to make the glaze spreadable.

When the cookies are cool, carefully spread the tops with glaze. Makes about 3½ dozen.

Sesame Crisps

Darlene, Allan, Walter and Athena Tansky   *Scarlett Point*

Both of the women on this lightstation cook on wood stoves. From their almost perfumed kitchens, they are constantly turning out cookies, breads and every other treat imaginable.

¼ cup	butter, at room temperature	50 mL
½ cup	brown sugar, lightly packed	125 mL
1	egg, beaten	1
½ tsp	vanilla	2 mL
½ cup	all-purpose flour	125 mL
½ tsp	baking powder	2 mL
½ cup	sesame seeds	125 mL

Preheat the oven to 375°F (190°C).

Cream the butter, sugar, egg and vanilla until fluffy. Stir together the flour and baking powder and add it to the creamed mixture. Mix in the sesame seeds thoroughly. Drop by teaspoonfuls onto a well-greased cookie sheet at least 2" (5 cm) apart. Bake for 10 minutes or until golden brown. Let cool on the pan for several minutes before removing. Cool completely and store in a tightly covered container.

Makes 2 dozen.

Ginger Cookies

Karen, John, Rod and Daniel Chungranes   *Entrance Island*

Soft and tender, these are among the most fragrant cookies you can bake.

⅔ cup	vegetable oil	150 mL
1 cup	granulated sugar	250 mL
1	egg, beaten	1
¼ cup	molasses	50 mL
2 cups	all-purpose flour	500 mL
2 tsps	baking soda	10 mL
¼ tsp	salt	1 mL
1 tsp	cinnamon	5 mL
1 tsp	ground ginger	5 mL
	additonal granulated sugar, as needed	

Preheat the oven to 350°F (180°C).

Whisk the oil and sugar together. Beat in the egg and molasses. In a separate bowl, combine the flour, soda, salt, cinnamon and ginger. Add to the first mixture and blend well. Shape the dough into 1″ (2.5 cm) balls and roll in granulated sugar. Place on lightly greased baking sheets and press down with a fork. Bake for 10–15 minutes or until the cookies have cracks in them.

Makes about 3 dozen.

Jumbo Raisin Cookies

Judy and Stan Westhaver   *Egg Island*

These cookies are very soft and moist.

2 cups	raisins	500 mL
1 cup	boiling water	250 mL
1 cup	shortening	250 mL
1¾ cups	granulated sugar	425 mL
3	eggs	3
2 tsps	vanilla	10 mL
4 cups	all-purpose flour	1 L
1 tsp	baking powder	5 ml
1 tsp	baking soda	5 mL
½ tsp	salt	2 mL
2 tsps	cinnamon	10 mL
½ tsp	ground cloves	2 mL

Cover the raisins with the boiling water and let stand until cool. Drain thoroughly.

Preheat the oven to 350°F (180°C).

Cream the shortening and sugar until fluffy. Add the eggs, one at a time, beating well after each. Whip in the vanilla. In a separate bowl, stir together the flour, baking powder, baking soda, salt and spices. Gradually add to the creamed mixture. Fold in the raisins. Drop by spoonfuls onto greased cookie sheets. Bake for 10–12 minutes.

Makes 3 dozen.

Cindy's Brown Sugar Drop Cookies

Cynthia, Dennis and Heather Rose   *Ivory Island*

Cynthia explains that she "goofed on another recipe and fixed it up in an attempt to save it. This is the result and now is our favourite—delicious little spicy pillows filled with raisins and nuts."

1 cup	milk	250 mL
2 tbsps	white vinegar	25 mL
1 cup	shortening	250 mL
2 cups	brown sugar	500 mL
2	eggs	2
1 tsp	vanilla	5 mL
3½ cups	all-purpose flour	875 mL
1 tsp	baking soda	5 mL
2 tsps	baking powder	10 mL
½ tsp	salt	2 mL
1 tsp	freshly grated nutmeg	5 mL
1 tsp	cinnamon	5 mL
½ tsp	ground ginger	2 mL
¾ cup	chocolate chips	175 mL
	and/or	
¾ cup	raisins	175 mL
	and/or	
½ cup	shredded coconut	125 mL
	and/or	
¾ cup	unsalted nuts	175 mL

Preheat the oven to 425°F (220°C).

Stir the milk and vinegar together and set aside to sour. Cream the shortening and brown sugar until fluffy. Add the eggs and vanilla, beating thoroughly.

Combine the flour, baking soda, baking powder, salt, nutmeg, cinnamon and ginger. Add the dry ingredients and the milk alternately to the creamed mixture until the batter is "fairly smooth and just firm enough to drop." Fold in any or all of the chocolate chips, raisins, coconut and nuts.

Drop by spoonfuls onto greased baking sheets. Bake in the centre of the oven for 10–12 minutes or until the cookie springs back when touched.

Makes about 4 dozen cookies.

Peanut Butter Delights

Judy and Stan Westhaver   *Egg Island*

My boys call these "Awesome!"

1 cup	peanut butter	250 mL
2 tbsps	softened butter	25 mL
1 cup	icing sugar	250 mL
1 tsp	vanilla	5 mL
1 cup	crispy rice cereal	250 mL
	maraschino cherries, as needed	
6 1 oz squares	semi-sweet chocolate	6 28 g squares

Cream the peanut butter, butter, icing sugar and vanilla. Add the cereal; mix thoroughly. Shape into small balls. Drain the cherries and poke one into the centre of each candy. Melt the chocolate in the top of a double boiler over simmering water. Using a fork, dip the cookies into the chocolate one at a time. Place on waxed paper to cool. Store, tightly covered, in the refrigerator.

Makes about 18 "delights."

Unbaked Chocolate Cookies

Wendy, Jim, Jessie and Melissa Abram   *Cape Mudge*

Fast and easy—fun for kids to whip up, then devour.

3 cups	quick-cooking oatmeal	750 mL
½ cup	cocoa	125 mL
1 cup	shredded coconut	250 mL
2 cups	granulated sugar	500 mL
½ cup	butter or margarine	125 mL
½ cup	milk	125 mL
1 tsp	vanilla	5 mL

Combine the oatmeal, cocoa and coconut in a medium-sized mixing bowl. Set aside.

Place the sugar, butter, milk and vanilla in a saucepan and bring to a boil over medium heat. Stir frequently to prevent sticking. Boil gently for 5 minutes. Remove from the heat and add the dry mixture immediately. Blend thoroughly. Drop the mixture by teaspoonfuls onto waxed paper. Chill before sampling.

Makes 3–4 dozen, depending on the size.

The Finishing Touch: Dessert and Candy

Pachena Point

Pumpkin Cheesecake

Cate Weir and Ian Crocker, Matthew and Peter   *Pachena Point*

Leaving well-paid positions (Cate was a French teacher) to take up lightkeeping was not an easy decision for Cate and Ian to make. But the lifestyle is one that really suits these two Renaissance people. Like many young keepers, they have made a conscious choice to leave the treadmill and realize their own potential as human beings. Cate bakes all of their bread, makes anything that she can from "scratch" and makes "cookies by the cart-load." They raise rabbits, cultivate a large organic garden, and harvest salal berries and wild crabapples for jellies.

Both Ian and Cate take part in educating their two small children. Every day, after lunch, Ian sits down to read to the boys. Cate has boxes of notes and the basement is the "science lab," where enormous polliwogs swim about in big jars.

Cate says that this cheesecake freezes well. If you love pumpkin pie, you'll love this smooth, spicy dessert.

Crumb Crust

1½ cups	graham cracker crumbs	375 mL
¼ cup	granulated sugar	50 mL
6 tbsps	melted butter	90 mL

Pumpkin Filling

3 8.8 oz pkgs	cream cheese	3 250 g pkgs
¾ cup	granulated sugar	175 ml
¾ cup	brown sugar	175 mL
5	eggs	5
½ tsp	ground cloves	2 mL
½ tsp	cinnamon	2 mL
½ tsp	mace	2 mL
½ tsp	freshly grated nutmeg	2 mL
1 16 oz tin	puréed pumpkin	1 455 mL tin
¼ cup	heavy cream (35%) or evaporated milk	50 mL

To prepare the crust, combine the crumbs, sugar and melted butter thoroughly. Pat into a 10" (25 cm) springform pan and set aside.

Preheat the oven to 325°F (160°C).

Beat the cheese until very smooth. Gradually whip in the sugar. Add the eggs, one at a time, beating well after each addition until light and fluffy. Stir in the cloves, cinnamon, mace, nutmeg, pumpkin and cream. Blend thoroughly. Pour into the prepared crust and bake for 1¾ hours. After baking, turn the oven off and leave the door ajar until the cheesecake cools.

Refrigerate until serving. Or cover tightly with plastic wrap and freeze. Before serving, garnish with whipped cream and a sprinkling of freshly grated nutmeg.

Makes 16 servings.

Wild Blackberry Pudding

Juanita and Vern Hills   *Green Island*

Located just south of the Alaska Panhandle, Green Island has no trees, but it does have lots of windblown grass and small, very brave shrubs. The trip in on the tough little zodiac was made even more exciting by the rather large swells. The landing was on wave-swept rocks and I had to jump and clamber as fast as possible to keep from being inundated by the freezing waters.

The island is so open that it receives a never-ending wind, hence a huge, rather loud wind generator constantly swishes and swirls.

No wild blackberries grow on Green Island, so Juanita, who the helicopter pilots say is one of the very best cooks in the northern district, journeyed to the mainland to pick the thorny canes. Juanita and Vern have recently been posted to an aeronautical beacon sight at Ethelda Bay, just off Prince Rupert, so blackberry picking will be much easier.

2–3 cups	wild blackberries or raspberries	500–750 mL
1½ cups	granulated sugar*	375 mL
½ cup	softened butter	125 mL
1	egg	1
½ tsp	salt	2 mL
1 cup	all-purpose flour	250 mL
1½ tsps	baking powder	7 mL
⅓ cup	milk	75 mL

*The amount of sugar may vary with the sweetness of the fruit used. Sprinkle an additional ¼ cup (50 mL) extra sugar if you are using tart fruits such as rhubarb.

Preheat the oven to 375°F (190°C).

Spread the berries evenly in a well-greased 9″ (22 cm) square glass baking dish. Sprinkle with 1 cup (250 mL) of the sugar.

Cream the butter, the remaining ½ cup (125 mL) sugar and the egg until light and fluffy. Stir together the salt, flour and baking powder. Add to the creamed mixture alternately with the milk. Spread the batter over the berries. Bake for 30 minutes or until the cake layer is done when tested with a toothpick. Wonderful served warm with milk or with cream, either plain or whipped.

Makes 6–8 servings.

Elaine's Apple Crisp

Elaine and Donald Graham   *Point Atkinson*

Apples are a staple on the lights. They can be stored for weeks "in the fridge or in a box on a cold porch or basement, so that lighthousekeepers, you always know you get your apple a day, one way or another."

¾ cup	granulated sugar	175 mL
1 tsp	cinnamon	5 mL
5–6	tart cooking apples, peeled and thinly sliced (Elaine prefers McIntosh or Granny Smiths)	5–6
1 cup	all-purpose flour	250 mL
½ cup	brown sugar	125 mL
½ cup	butter	125 mL
½ cup	rolled oats	125 mL

Preheat the oven to 375°F (190°C).

Combine the sugar and cinnamon. Toss with the apples and arrange in a buttered 2 qt (2 L) casserole.

Blend the flour and brown sugar. Coarsely cut in the butter with a fork or pastry blender. Stir in the oatmeal and sprinkle evenly over the apples.

Bake, uncovered, for 40–45 minutes or until the apples are tender and the topping is bubbling and brown.

Serve warm with table cream and leave the casserole in the centre of the table for second helpings!

Makes about 4 servings.

Homemade Chocolate Pudding

Wendy, Jim, Jessie and Melissa Abram   *Cape Mudge*

Her jeans are patched with a bit of flowered corduroy, her plaid bush jacket is buttoned with bone, the flowing mane of curly hair frames her easy smile and when she talks she expresses her feelings with her graceful hands. Wendy Abram is a natural beauty.

She uses this recipe a lot—it's easy and quick and it makes delicious chocolate pies.

½ cup	granulated sugar	125 mL
⅓ cup	cornstarch	75 mL
¼ tsp	salt	1 mL
⅓ cup	cocoa	75 mL
2½ cups	milk	625 mL

| 1½ tsps | vanilla | 7 mL |

Stir the dry ingredients together in a heavy saucepan. Gradually blend in the milk and cook over medium heat, stirring constantly, until the pudding begins to thicken and bubble. Cook 2–3 minutes longer. Remove from the heat and add the vanilla. Immediately pour into a large serving bowl or 4 dessert dishes. Cool to room temperature and refrigerate until well chilled.

Microwave Variation

Combine the dry ingredients in a 2 quart (2 L) microwave-safe casserole. Whisk in the milk and microwave on High for 8–10 minutes, stirring and turning the bowl 3 or 4 times. When thickened, add the vanilla and proceed as above.

Spanish Rice Pudding

Judy and Stan Westhaver   *Egg Island*

Judy says that she doubles this recipe and they still clean it all up. She uses powdered skim milk instead of whole milk: it's easier for them to store. I like to toss in a handful of raisins at the same time as the vanilla is added.

1 quart	milk*	1 L
1	cinnamon stick	1
2 2″ strips	lemon rind, yellow part only	2 5 cm strips
2 2″ strips	orange rind, orange part only	2 5 cm strips
1 cup	uncooked short grain rice	250 mL
2 cups	water	500 mL
⅔ cup	granulated sugar	150 mL
1/4 tsp	vanilla	1 mL
	cinnamon, as needed	

*Either use whole milk or reconstitute 1⅓ cups (325 mL) instant skim milk powder with 3¾ cups (925 mL) cold water to yield about 1 quart (1 L).

Place the milk, cinnamon stick, lemon and orange rinds in a large, heavy saucepan. Heat gently over low heat until the mixture begins to simmer. At the same time, parboil the rice in the water for 5 minutes. Drain well. When the milk boils, add the rice. Simmer, "with the lid askew," for 15 minutes, stirring now and then. Stir in the sugar and continue to cook 15–20 minutes longer or until most of the liquid is absorbed and the rice is very soft. Remove the cinnamon stick, lemon and orange rinds. Stir in the vanilla. Pour into a well-buttered 1 quart (1 L) casserole. Sprinkle the top with ground cinnamon. Cool, then chill for several hours before serving.

Makes 4–6 servings.

Tryphina's Apple Dumplings

Judy and Stan Westhaver   *Egg Island*

Judy says, "My mother-in-law is a terrific cook, besides being a marvellous lady. This is one of the things she fills our freezer with when she comes to visit. Together we spend our days shell hunting on the beach, quilting, me learning various crafts and she doing the patient teaching; talking and solving the world's problems while we cook."

| 9 | large cooking apples, peeled and cored | 9 |

Syrup

2¼ cups	granulated sugar	550 mL
3 cups	water	750 mL
1 tbsp	cinnamon	15 mL
1 tsp	freshly grated nutmeg	5 mL
¾ cup	butter	175 mL

Pastry

3 cups	all-purpose flour	750 mL
3 tsps	baking powder	15 mL
½ tsp	salt	2 mL
1¼ cups	lard	300 mL
¾ cup	milk	175 mL

Preheat the oven to 375°F (190°C).

Prepare the syrup by combining the sugar, water and spices and bringing them to a boil in a small saucepan. Whisk in the butter and remove from the heat. Set aside while making the pastry.

Combine the flour, baking powder and salt in a large mixing bowl. Cut in the lard with a pastry blender until the mixture has the appearance of fine crumbs. Add the milk all at once, stirring to blend evenly. Knead into a ball.

Cut the dough into two equal pieces. On a lightly floured surface, roll each piece into two 12" x 16" (30 x 40 cm) rectangles. Lay the apple pieces lengthwise along the middle of each. Bring the edges of the pastry up over the apples, pinching to seal. Place the rolls in separate 9" x 13" (3.5 L) ungreased baking dishes. Pour half the syrup over each roll. Bake for 35–40 minutes or until the dumplings are golden brown and bubbling.

Makes 8–10 servings.

Green Island

Fruit Kanten

Lee Wehrwein-Gilbert and John Gilbert, Matthew, Sasha and Oban   *Ballenas Island*

This recipe is for a refreshing and very low-calorie dessert based on Kanten, a gelatin made from the sea vegetable agar-agar. It can be purchased in translucent bars in many Japanese or health food stores that specialize in macrobiotic cooking. Shave or crush the bars into almost any liquid and pour it over fruit or vegetables. It sets at room temperature.

This is a very basic recipe that can be easily altered by using different fruits or liquids. I thawed some frozen strawberries and pureed them, threw in some orange juice and used extra whole berries in one of my latest variations.

4 cups	apple juice	1 L
1 1½ oz pkg	kanten	1 15 g pkg
3	apples or pears, peeled, cored and thinly sliced	3

Heat the juice in a small saucepan. Tear or shred the bars of kanten into the juice. Stir to dissolve while it heats. Arrange the apple or pear slices attractively in a glass bowl or in individual serving dishes. Pour the hot juice over and allow it to cool at room temperature. Refrigerate if you are not serving it immediately.

Makes 4–6 servings.

Judy's Fabulous Butterscotch Fudge

Judy and Stan Westhaver   *Egg Island*

It melts in your mouth!

1 cup	walnut pieces	250 mL
1 6 oz pkg	butterscotch chips	1 170 g pkg
1 tsp	vanilla	5 mL
½ cup	butter	125 mL
2 cups	granulated sugar	500 mL
¾ cup	·evaporated milk	175 mL
10	large marshmallows	10

Combine the walnuts, butterscotch chips and vanilla in a mixing bowl. Put the butter, sugar, evaporated milk and marshmallows into a heavy saucepan. Bring to a boil over medium heat, stirring constantly. Boil for 6 minutes, timing carefully. Pour over the walnut mixture, and stir until the chips are dissolved. Pour into a buttered 8" (20 cm) square pan. Cool and cut into squares.

Makes 64 1" (2.5 cm) pieces.

Christmas Glazed Almonds

Judy and Stan Westhaver   *Egg Island*

It's difficult for Judy to find delicious treats that are easy to ship to friends across the water. These glazed almonds are perfect. She always makes several large batches and "does them up in fancy containers."

1 cup	whole blanched almonds	250 mL
½ cup	granulated sugar	125 mL
2 tbsps	butter	25 mL
½ tsp	vanilla	2 mL

Combine the almonds, sugar and butter in a heavy skillet (cast iron is great, but Judy uses her electric frying pan). Cook over medium heat, stirring constantly for about 10 minutes or until the almonds are toasted and the sugar is golden brown. Stir in the vanilla. Spread the nuts on a sheet of aluminum foil.

Cool and then break into chunks with a fork.

Makes 1 cup (250 mL) glazed nuts.

Glazed Spiced Nuts

Judy and Stan Westhaver   *Egg Island*

Judy makes this spicy treat at Christmas time to ship to friends and relatives. There is one caution that should be noted — they are addictive!

¾ cup	granulated sugar	175 mL
¾ tsp	salt	4 mL
1 tsp	cinnamon	5 mL
½ tsp	ground cloves	2 mL
¼ tsp	allspice	1 mL
¼ tsp	nutmeg	1 mL
1	egg white, slightly beaten	1
2½ tbsps	water	30 mL
1 cup	walnut halves	250 mL
1 cup	pecan halves	250 mL
1 cup	brazil nuts	250 mL

Preheat the oven to 275°F (140°C).

Combine the sugar, salt, cinnamon, cloves, allspice and nutmeg. Stir in the egg white and water until blended. Add the nuts ½ cup (125 mL) at a time, stirring with a fork till coated. Lift the nuts out of the syrup one by one and place them on a greased baking sheet, side by side. Bake for 35–45 minutes or until golden and crusty. Cool and store in a tightly covered container. (Hide them until serving.)

Makes 3 cups (750 mL).

Fluffy Rum Sauce

Gwen and Doug Fraser   *Pine Island*

Gwen has been making this sauce for thirty years, for her Christmas Pudding. The recipe was handed down to her by Doug's mother who has had it for as long as she can remember.

½ cup	butter	125 mL
2 cups	icing sugar	500 mL
3 tbsps	rum ("Or more if you'd like," says Gwen)	45 mL
4	eggs, separated	4
1 cup	table cream (18%)	250 mL

In the top of a double boiler, cream the butter and icing sugar. Add the rum slowly. Beat the egg yolks well and pour into the rum mixture. Whisk in the cream. Place over simmering water and cook, stirring, until the sauce thickens. In a separate bowl, beat the egg whites until very stiff. Slowly pour in the hot sauce, beating constantly. Serve immediately, and refrigerate any that may be left over. When re-using the refrigerated sauce, stir well before serving.

Makes about 4 cups (1 L) fluffy sauce.

Index